STORIES
From a
WISE
WOMAN

Who Dared to Believe God and His Word

VICKIE WOOTEN

Trilogy Christian Publishers
A Wholly Owned Subsidiary of Trinity Broadcasting Network
2442 Michelle Drive
Tustin, CA 92780

Cover design by: Cornerstone Creative Solutions

For information, address Trilogy Christian Publishing
Rights Department, 2442 Michelle Drive, Tustin, Ca 92780.
Trilogy Christian Publishing/ TBN and colophon are trademarks of Trinity Broadcasting Network.

For information about special discounts for bulk purchases, please contact Trilogy Christian Publishing.

Manufactured in the United States of America

10 9 8 7 6 5 4 3 2 1

Library of Congress Cataloging-in-Publication Data is available.

ISBN 978-1-64773-674-3 (Print Book)
ISBN 978-1-64773-675-0 (ebook)

DEDICATION

This book is dedicated to my mother Pearl, my son Nathan, my daughter Teri, and my grandchildren.

CONTENTS

FOREWORD

We have to remember that our number one purpose is to win souls for the kingdom. We have an enemy that wants to destroy us and derail the plans, purpose, and destiny that our Father has for us. I grew up hearing these stories over and over my entire life, but it is stories like these that increase our faith. The purpose of the book is to help increase your faith, and we pray that the Holy Spirit will reveal truth to you. We pray that you will have your own supernatural spiritual experiences so you will never be able to deny the existence of God—our Creator, our Father. He loves us and is patient with us—wishing none to perish, but all to repent and come back home to Him (2 Peter 3:9). We pray that you will walk in confidence, knowing your identity as a child of God, loved by your Father, who desires nothing more than to be in a relationship with you. We pray that God will give you opportunities to share your stories and that you will walk in righteousness and speak boldly for the Lord. It is not our job to convince people that anything or anyone is real or true; the Holy Spirit will draw their hearts to Him and reveal the truth. It is our job to simply be obedient and tell our stories and plant the seeds.

My mom has the ability to turn any conversation into one about the Lord. She is one of the most loving, compassionate people I've ever known. I grew up listening to her talk to people, always telling them about the Lord, telling what He has done for her, offering to pray with them. I was always so proud of her walk with the Lord and hoped that one day God would use me as He used her. My gifts are different from hers. He doesn't use me in the exact same ways, but I am so thankful for a Godly inheritance. She was a single mom working several jobs and raising two kids. We didn't have a lot of material things, but she knew what was truly important in life. She loved us, told us about the Lord, kept us in church, and taught us to believe that anything is possible with God.—Teri (Vickie's daughter)

> Therefore we do not lose heart. Though outwardly we are wasting away, yet inwardly we are being renewed day by day. For our light and momentary troubles are achieving for us an eternal glory that far outweighs them all. So we fix our eyes not on what is seen, but on what is unseen, since what is seen is temporary, but what is unseen is eternal.
> 2 Corinthians 4:16-18 (NIV)

PREFACE

M y first story begins with my mother Pearl, who was a rare and beautiful pearl. She was born in 1919 into a large southern family. She never got to attend a school or learn to read or write. She was the second oldest child and had to care for the others as her parents worked on the farm. All of her life, she loved going to church, where she found her peace and her joy. As a child, she walked us to whatever church was close enough to walk to. We never missed a service. This little five-foot-two-inch woman never read the Word of God but lived it every day. She loved everyone. She had a servant's heart. She birthed and raised twelve kids and put a faith in them that the world and the devil couldn't take out of them. Some of them took their time coming to know Jesus, but they all got there. I remember hearing her pray and seeing God answer. She would tell us there was nothing that God could not do for us and nothing that He would not do for us. She taught me to believe, and I would not be the woman of faith that I am today without her, so all of my stories are connected to her, my precious Pearl. What a gift she was to all who knew her!

VICKIE WOOTEN

FAITH AND MIRACLES

One of the stories from my mother happened long before I was born. She was a young mother. She had fallen and injured her back real bad. She was a free bleeder and had had a slow bleed for almost five years. She had internal injuries, and her womb was apparently tilted. She did not get pregnant during those five years. (She had a baby or a miscarriage every eighteen months to two years until her childbearing years were over. She had twelve kids and two known miscarriages). She kept getting weaker day by day until she could not get up out of bed. My father had a drinking and gambling problem and wasn't taking care of her. Her mother had passed away from cancer and left her with several young siblings to raise, and she had three young children of her own at that time. They lived in a small town in Alabama. There was no hospital nearby. My dad went and got a country doctor when he saw that she couldn't get up out of bed. The doctor told her that she had bled to the point of death, and there was nothing he could do. He walked out of the room. She closed her eyes and began to pray. She prayed to Jesus and told Him, "There's nobody to raise these children if I die. Please let me live to raise these children." She opened her eyes, and Jesus Christ was there standing in the corner of her bedroom. She said He looked just like the pictures. He didn't speak or touch her. He looked at her and smiled, and she felt healing go from the hairs of her head all through her body. He left the room. He had to have replaced the blood in her body. She got up and cooked supper and went on with life. She birthed nine more children and raised them all. She raised countless grandchildren. At the time of her death in 1989, she had fifty plus grandchildren and great-grandchildren and was ready to go meet her Lord.

> "All things are possible for one who believes" (Mark 9:23 ESV).

ANOTHER MAMA MIRACLE

In 1970, mama got sick and started throwing up blood. Because she was a free bleeder and had a rare blood type, someone had to get on the radio and beg people to come in and give blood for her. They were giving her blood, but it was just pooling up in her stomach. The doctor said there was so much blood in her stomach that they were pumping it off, but it was just filling back up. The doctor decided it was stomach cancer or bleeding ulcers. There was too much blood for them to see what it was. She was too weak for surgery, and they couldn't stop the bleeding, so they called the family in and told us it would just be a matter of hours. I wasn't a Christian at the time, but I was trying to pray. Her little church came and gathered in the intensive care waiting room and got on their knees and prayed. They prayed Ezekiel 16:6. I have always heard that if you pray it in faith three times, it will stop bleeding, and it did. She immediately improved, and her doctor said to her, "Woman, you have the strongest will to live of anyone I've ever seen, or there is a higher power somewhere." She said, "Doctor, there is definitely a higher power." Within a few days, she went home from the hospital and went on with her life. In 1985 she started having stomach trouble again. My sister, who was an RN, took her to one of our local doctors who put a light and a camera in her stomach. When he looked into her stomach, he was upset that they had not listed her surgery on her chart. There were no previous surgeries listed on her paperwork. He asked her how they did the surgery on her stomach because there was no outer scar. She said, "Doctor, I've never had stomach surgery." He said, "I see the perfect stitches where one-third of your stomach has been removed, and I want to know how they did the surgery." She again said, "Doctor, I've never had any stomach surgery." Then he turned to my sister, who he knew was an RN, and said, "Tell me how they did this surgery. I see the perfect stitches where one-third of her stomach has been removed." My sister assured him that she had never had stomach surgery, and my mother said, "Well, God himself had to have done it fifteen years ago when I was having bleeding problems." They left a bewildered doctor that day.

My mother's name was Pearl. She was a pearl of great price, a beautiful woman of God, and a great example of His love and mercy.

> "Behold, I am the LORD, the God of all flesh. Is there anything too hard for Me?" (Jeremiah 32:27 ESV)

> "And he said unto her, Daughter, thy faith hath made thee whole; go in peace and be whole of thy plague" (Mark 5:34 KJV).

> "Is any sick among you? let him call for the elders of the church; and let them pray over him, anointing him with oil in the name of the Lord: And the prayer of faith shall save the sick, and the Lord shall raise him up; and if he have com-

mitted sins, they shall be forgiven him" (James 5:14-15 KJV).

"Who forgiveth all thine iniquities; who healeth all thy diseases" (Psalm 103:3 KJV).

"So shall my word be that goeth forth out of my mouth: it shall not return unto me void, but it shall accomplish that which I please, and it shall prosper in the thing whereto I sent it" (Isaiah 55:11 KJV).

"He that followeth after righteousness and mercy findeth life, righteousness, and honour" (Proverbs 21:21 KJV).

MY FIRST ENCOUNTER
WITH GOD

My first memory of God connecting with me was when I was between five and six years old. We lived in an old farmhouse in Lafayette, Georgia, with too many kids and not enough beds. I was sleeping with my older sister Mary. I woke up to people talking and music in our bedroom. We didn't have a TV or a radio that I remember. I was sleeping behind my sister's back, and it was cold. I was snuggled up to her, and I saw a scene like a movie in our bedroom. I was scared, and I didn't understand why my sister didn't wake up. There was a man and a woman. They were dressed strangely. Everything in the room in the scene that I saw was different from anything I had ever seen before. I snuggled down behind my sister's back, afraid and thinking that if they didn't see me, they wouldn't know that I was there. The scene went away, and I went back to sleep. I don't remember telling anyone about it. I didn't understand what a vision was. When I was twenty-seven years old, I walked into that scene in a German restaurant. I asked myself, "Why did God give me that vision when I was a little girl?" I think He wanted me to know that my going there with my husband in the military was part of His plan and that when I got there, I would know that it was Him who had given me the vision. He was working in my life when I didn't even know how to acknowledge Him. God did so very much for me during our two tours of Germany. I met my spiritual parents on the first trip, who took me under their arms and taught me how to walk with the Lord and so many wonderful parenting skills. Father God placed so many amazing brothers and sisters in the Lord in my life on both tours.

> You watched me as I was being formed in utter seclusion, as I was woven together in the dark of the womb. You saw me before I was born. Every day of my life was recorded in your book. Every moment was laid out before a single day had passed. How precious are your thoughts about me, O God. They cannot be numbered! I can't even count them; they outnumber the grains of sand! And when I wake up, you are still with me!
>
> Psalm 139:15-18 (NLT)

MY FIRST *REAL* ENCOUNTER WITH GOD

When I was seven years old, we lived in Alva, Florida. We went to a tiny church in the Alva community. I remember one Sunday night service at the end of the service when the pastor was giving the altar call, I felt God pulling me toward the altar, trying to urge me to go. There were people in the altar area doing things that I didn't understand, and the kids around me were making fun of them. A part of me wanted to go to the altar, but I didn't want the kids making fun of me. The pastor asked us to stand, and my feet began to walk away from my body against my will. I held on to the back of the pew with all my strength, and my feet walked as far as they could go without pulling me down. I felt I was about to be pulled in two, and God turned loose. He knew that I would never forget and that I would know it was Him. I have many times regretted that I did not go forward that night. I was 24 when I finally gave my heart to God. All through the years, I could feel Him tugging at me, and He gave me dreams. After I became a Christian and began to witness, whenever I would encounter people who said they didn't believe in God, I would tell them that I could take them to the place that God made Himself real to me when I was seven. I knew it was God, and I knew He wanted me. At sixty-one years old,

I went back to Alva, Florida, and found that church and went inside, and I found my spot. I told the pastor that day my story, and I hope he is still telling it because we have a God who will go to any length to reach us.

> "For the Son of Man came to seek and save those who are lost" (Luke 19:10 NLT).

THE HEALER IS A PRAYER AWAY

The summer that I was seven, when we lived in the little town of Alva, Florida, we were running through the weeds near our house one day and near the sawmill where my dad worked. We were all barefoot. I stepped on a little oval flat type jar. It broke and cut my right foot about half off. We lived thirty-five miles from a hospital and did not have a car. The only thing we had to kill germs was kerosene. My mom prayed and poured kerosene all over my foot and then cleaned my foot up, wrapped it in a clean cloth, propped my foot up on the end of the sofa, and sent two of the kids down to the church about three blocks away to get the preacher. The preacher and a deacon came and anointed me with oil and prayed. That was all that was ever done for my foot. It never got infected, and I've never had a problem with it. The big scars are still there. Our God always comes through.

> "Yet, Lord my God, give attention to your servant's prayer and his plea for mercy. Hear the cry and the prayer that your servant is praying in your presence" (2 Chronicles 6:19 NIV).

"Don't worry about anything; instead, pray about everything. Tell God what you need, and thank him for all he has done" (Philippians 4:6 NLT).

WITHOUT HOPE

At ten years old, we lived in a big old farmhouse with a barn and acreage. It was one of my favorite places to live growing up. One day I sat on the back porch, and I was looking out over the garden spot, and I was thinking, *I'm never going to live to be an adult.* I would hear people say, "When I grow up, I'm going to be this or I'm going to do that." I wasn't doing well in school, and I didn't think there was anything in life that I could do or do well, so I had no hope, and I didn't feel like I had a future. I didn't know God then, and I had no idea that He has a plan for all of us. I didn't finish school or have a career. At sixty-eight years old, I can say that life was very, very hard at times. I surrendered to God at twenty-four years old. My life had already sustained a lot of damage by then. God has blessed me, and His fingerprints are all over my life. It's been quite a journey. It took me a lot of years to trust God after I was saved. I didn't feel like I could trust anyone, but God I found to be trustworthy. It took me way too long to get there. Take the shortcut. Believe what the Word says completely.

> "For I know the plans I have for you, declares the Lord, plans to prosper you and not to harm you, plans to give you hope and a future" (Jeremiah 29:11 NIV).

25

CLOSE ENCOUNTER

When we lived in the old farmhouse down in the country, I was ten. It was summer. It was Sunday afternoon. We had family over, and everyone was out on the front porch. I had taken two small nieces and had walked them down the road from our house. I could hear my family on the front porch, but there was a little hill, and I couldn't see them, and they couldn't see me. I was ten, but I looked fourteen or fifteen. I had matured early. A car pulled up, and two guys tried to get me to go for a ride with them in the car. I told them no, and they became insistent. I realized that I was in danger and that they might try to force me into the car. I know it was God who put the words in my mouth and the idea in my head. I know it couldn't have come from my ten-year-old mind. I said to the two men, "I have to take these kids back to the house, or I will get in trouble. I'll come back and meet you in an hour." They left, and I know I didn't think that up on my own. I was on the porch with my family, and they did come back by. I never went walking by myself again. I know God probably saved my life that day. If I had gone with them, I probably never would have seen my family again. I thank God for that miracle.

> "I will lift up mine eyes unto the hills,
> from whence cometh my help. My help
> comes from the Lord, which made heaven
> and earth" (Psalm 121:1-2 KJV).

A Proud Daughter

When I was eleven, my oldest sister Ruby and her three boys had moved in with us in the old farmhouse. Since we lived in the country, we never got to go to any school sports or functions. My mother never drove. One of my sister's sons was going to be in a PTA program, so she took some of us along and took our mom. I always thought my mother was such a beautiful woman. No one at school had ever seen her, so I was so proud that I got to go to PTA and that people in my class could see my mother because I was so proud of her. She was a little five-foot-two-inch round American Indian lady who always made her own dresses. I only knew of her buying one dress from a store. It was a beautiful memory from my childhood.

> Charm and grace are deceptive, and [superficial] beauty is vain,
> But a woman who fears the Lord [reverently worshiping, obeying, serving, and trusting Him with awe-filled respect], she shall be praised.
>
> Proverbs 31:30 (AMP)

VICKIE WOOTEN

BE CAREFUL OF THE WORDS YOU SPEAK, WORDS CAN WOUND PEOPLE SO DEEPLY

At eleven years old, I went home with a friend one weekend, just for the day. We usually were not allowed to go to people's homes. I had gone to school with this girl for at least two years, and her half-brother had married one of my sisters, so my mom let them take me over there for the day. The other little girl and I had been outside playing. We were going in for a snack or a drink, and she was a little way ahead of me. She had gone into the house first, and I came up to the screen door and put my hand on the handle about to go in, and I heard her mother say, "Don't bring that girl home with you anymore. Any girl that has a body that looks like that at age eleven has been doing bad things that she shouldn't be doing." I didn't have a good understanding of what that meant. Her daughter was the same age as me and had no shape or form yet, and was being molested by her step-brother all the time. He had talked to her and asked her to ask me if he could have sex with me. I didn't fully understand any of that, but I knew it wasn't anything I needed to do, and I didn't, but her mother's words haunted me for years.

We can't help how our bodies mature, but it does not have anything to do with our sexual activity. Through the years, I would wonder, "Does everyone who looks at me think that I've been a bad girl doing bad things?" That was very painful for years, so be careful what you speak over others. Guard the words you speak over and around children.

> "The Lord detests the thoughts of the wicked, but gracious words are pure in his sight" (Proverbs 15:26 NIV).

> "Bear with each other and forgive one another if any of you has a grievance against someone. Forgive as the Lord forgave you" (Colossians 3:13 NIV).

Loosed from the Grip of the Enemy

My life from age twelve to twenty-four was filled with pain and tragedy. My teenage years were the worst of my life. I prayed to die day after day. I seemed to make one wrong decision after another. Finally, at age twenty-four, I decided that I would end my life. I have a precious sister-in-law who loved me, prayed for me, and reached out to me continually. If I needed something, she was always there (and forty-four years later, she still is). I cut my wrist. I'm not a free bleeder like my mom, but I bleed more than normal. I cut both wrists with a dirty, rusty old razor blade that had been in my sewing box for years. As soon as I did it, I thought, *Oh my God, what if my mother is the one to find me. This will kill her.* I was lost as a duck in the desert, but I started praying for God to help my mama through my death, and then the bleeding stopped. I cut back through my wrists again, but they would not bleed. I didn't know what to do, so I called that little sister-in-law who is a spiritual giant. It took her two weeks, but she finally got me to go to church, and I surrendered to the love and forgiveness of Jesus. I still made my share of mistakes—a failed second marriage. But aside from my salvation, God gave me the two most wonderful gifts—my son and my daughter. They gave me a reason to live and have blessed my life daily.

I now have nine grandchildren of whom I'm so proud. I'm so thankful God didn't let me die that day. I would have missed so very much. Look what the devil tried to cheat me out of through all of his lies, and I've had the opportunity to lead quite a few people to Jesus. I am blessed. All praise, honor, and glory go to Jesus—my Savior, Kinsman Redeemer, my Lord, my King, my Deliverer, my Everything. I could not, nor would I want to live one moment without Him.

> Be gracious to me, O God, according to Your lovingkindness; According to the greatness of Your compassion blot out my transgressions. Wash me thoroughly from my iniquity and cleanse me from my sin. For I know my transgressions, and my sin is ever before me. Against You, You only, I have sinned and done what is evil in Your sight, so that You are justified when You speak and blameless when You judge. Behold, I was brought forth in iniquity, and in sin my mother conceived me. Behold, You desire truth in the innermost being, and in the hidden part, You will make me know wisdom. Purify me with hyssop, and I shall be clean; Wash me, and I shall be whiter than snow. Make me to hear joy and gladness, Let the bones which You have broken rejoice. Hide Your face from my sins and blot out all my iniquities. Create in me a clean heart, O God, and renew a steadfast spirit within me. Do not cast

me away from Your presence and do not take Your Holy Spirit from me.

Psalm 51:1-11 (NASB)

One thing I have asked from the Lord, that I shall seek: That I may dwell in the house of the Lord all the days of my life, to behold the beauty of the Lord and to meditate in His temple. For in the day of trouble He will conceal me in His tabernacle; In the secret place of His tent He will hide me; He will lift me up on a rock. And now my head will be lifted up above my enemies around me, and I will offer in His tent sacrifices with shouts of joy; I will sing, yes, I will sing praises to the Lord.

Psalm 27:4-6 (NASB)

How blessed is the man who does not walk in the counsel of the wicked, nor stand in the path of sinners, nor sit in the seat of scoffers! But his delight is in the law of the Lord, and in His law, he meditates day and night.

Psalm 1:1-2 (NASB)

MY RUNAWAY
SUMMER 1975

My first marriage went through a devastating weekend.
We had been married for a while, with no children and a
lot of struggles. I was in my early twenties and did not drive
yet. I didn't think I was smart enough to drive. I also didn't
finish school, but I had a good job. I had a broken marriage,
so I decided I needed to get away. My mom talked me into
visiting my brother, who lived in another state. I stayed a
few days, but I didn't want to be a burden on his family. I
got on the bus and went one hour north of my brother. I
got a newspaper and walked to the only job in the paper.
There was a men's boarding house but nothing in the paper
to rent—no women's boarding house, so I went on to the
job. The man said, "Why should I give you this job? There
are people who live here who need it." It was on a Friday. He
said, "If I give you this job, I don't even know if you will be
here on Monday. You don't even have a place to live." I said,
"I need this job. I want to live here, and I will make you a
good employee. If you give me a job, I'll find a place to live
and be here on Monday morning to work." He gave me the
job. I walked about three blocks up the street, and there was
a man doing yard work on the corner. I asked him if he knew
anyone who rented any rooms in that area or had a small

apartment. He said, "Wait right here. I'll be right back," and he was. He said, "Come with me. I want you to meet the lady who lives here." She was seventy-five and lived alone in a big two-story house. Her daughter lived an hour away and would bring her yardman when she came to visit. He told her that he had found her someone perfect to stay with her mother and that I was a trustworthy person. They took his word and rented me the upstairs of the house with kitchen and laundry privileges. I spent the summer there with this precious lady. We took a cab to church, shopping, and occasionally out to eat. It was a great experience. Her family was very kind to me and took me on a few family outings. To their disappointment, I went back to my husband and home. That was a big mistake followed by a divorce and more mistakes, but I found a real relationship with Jesus a year later. I married again. Again, another journey with many ups and downs and wrong decisions. We traveled a lot with the army and had two children. Twelve years later, we divorced. I am not saying that we should not have married, but we should have dated longer and gotten to know each other better. We each had been through a lot. I highly recommend three months of marriage counseling with a very knowledgeable pastor before getting married. It would save many marriages. It's very important that we seek God when we are making decisions. I didn't always know just how to. Pray and seek. The Word says, "Seek and you will find, knock and the door will be opened to you" (Matthew 7:7 NIV). I live by that verse now.

DREAMS

Even as a lost person, I had dreams with meaning and premonition. I married my first husband when I was very young. All of us girls married early to get away from our dad—a man with many demons. One night, I had a dream that my husband was lying on his back, dead with a gunshot to his chest. He was wearing his Sunday clothes. We didn't go to church, but for some reason, we dressed up for Sundays. I don't remember what day I dreamed it on, but the next Sunday, one of my sister's husbands was found shot dead in the chest. I never understood why I dreamed that, but I also dreamed of my daughter while I was in that marriage. I didn't have any children with my first husband, but I was praying for a little girl, and I had a dream about her. In the dream, I had left her in the hospital room with family and went to get coffee. When I came back, she was covered with a sheet. They told me she was dead. She looked to be about two years old. When I pulled back the sheet, she was alive and looked at me and smiled. I woke up and thought, "What a crazy dream." When my little girl was two and looked just like that little girl in the dream, the Lord showed me that dream again as I stepped from my kitchen one day into the living room. It was like looking at a big movie screen, and I said, "Oh Lord, are you about to take her away from me?" He said, "No, you were dead to me in your sins when you asked me for her, and when you came alive to me, didn't I give you what you asked for? I wanted you to know that I was listening back then." I want you all to know that I'm thankful for God's timing. His timing is better than ours. When I remarried and was expecting, I asked the Lord to give me a son first so my daughter would have a big brother to care for her, and He graciously did. Our God is a mighty, wise, and wonderful God.

> "This is the confidence we have in approaching God: that if we ask anything according to his will, he hears us" (1 John 5:14 NIV).

> "Look at the nations and watch—and be utterly amazed. For I am going to do something in your days that you would not believe, even if you were told" (Habakkuk 1:5 NIV).

NATHAN'S BIRTH
MARCH 1978

I had a perfect pregnancy with my first child. We were stationed at Fort Gordon in the Augusta, Georgia area—our first duty station when our son was born. A few days before his birth, I was kind of miserable, which is normal when you are nine months pregnant. I was thinking about my mom and missing her so badly. I just felt I needed her. We had no phone. We lived out in the country away from the base. I was washing dishes and crying for my mom at twenty-six years old when I heard a car door. One of my sisters brought my mom down to spend a week with me. It was unusual for her to leave home. She was always babysitting grandkids, but she knew I needed her. I was overjoyed.

We had a revival that week at our little country church, so we had been going every night. I was always up at 6 a.m. when my husband got up, and we didn't get home until 9 p.m. from the church. That Friday night, as soon as we got home, my water broke. I took a fresh shower, and then we headed for the hospital—no labor pains yet. The little one was on the way. They checked me and got me prepped. I was dilated to three, but no pains yet. I had been up since 6 a.m., and at midnight they decided that I would not have the baby until the next day. They gave me a pill and a shot and told me that I would rest and have the baby the next day. Well, five minutes later, I went into labor. The medicines they gave me knocked the baby and me out. As the pain increased, it would wake me up enough to cry out, and they would get upset with me for that, but I couldn't respond. I remember through the early morning them trying to get me awake enough to push him out and them saying that I was dilated to eight and I needed to push, but I couldn't. They kept saying, "Your baby is ready. We can see the head and hair. You've got to wake up and push." The pains were bad, and I had not taken Lamaze class because the classes were too far from us, and we didn't have the gas money to go. At about 8:30 a.m., they let my white-faced husband and my mother in. They were praying I would push the baby out. He was so drugged that he could not push himself out. My mom got me awake enough to start pushing. My husband went and called his mom to pray. They couldn't do a c-section because he was too far down. After two and a half hours of pushing, it felt like my eyes were going to pop out, and my temples felt like they would burst from my blood pressure being so high. They cut me as far as possible and pulled him out with forceps. He was eight pounds and twenty-one inches long—a healthy, precious baby boy. He couldn't wake up enough to eat for five days. My blood pressure was up for weeks. I hemorrhaged until they wouldn't let me up or move for eight hours. Then they threw me into a room with four other moms and treated us like soldiers. We had to get up and get our babies the first twenty-four hours at the nursery, feed them, change them, and carry them back. We had to go get our food trays and take them back down the hall. We had to go get clean sheets and gowns and change our beds and take the dirty linens back down the hall. We got no rest.

They made us go to classes on motherhood, and we were required to take an exercise class before we left the hospital on the third day. Then the doctor came into the room and was talking to a lady across the room. We could hear everything. He was talking to her about her high blood pressure and how she should have been on bed rest, but that didn't get on her chart (the entire three days), and for that, he was sorry, but they felt they should keep her a couple of more days. She got upset and said she didn't have high blood pressure. Then he looked and realized he had the wrong patient. He came over to me and said, "Well, you heard what I told her. I guess you need to stay a couple more days." I said, "No, I need to go home. I think I'll rest better there." They never told me how high my blood pressure was or treated it in any way. It was bad for weeks. I would get dizzy, and I could feel the blood through my temples, the back of my head, and spine. It was painful. I didn't know what to do. When I went back after six weeks, it was fine. I said I would never birth another baby in an army hospital, and I didn't. The next one was born in a parking garage, but not on purpose. I thank God for praying mamas, or we would not have made it.

> "Give praise to the Lord, proclaim his name; make known among the nations what he has done. Sing to him, sing praise to him; tell of all his wonderful acts" (Psalm 105:1-2 NIV).

> "My help comes from the Lord, the Maker of heaven and earth" (Psalm 121:2 NIV).

GOD HAS OUR BACKS

My husband was stationed in Mannheim, Germany, from 1978–1979. I took our one-year-old son and got on a plane for the first time in my life. It was a rough trip. We first flew from Atlanta to New York. I ran through the airport in heels. We took off late in Atlanta and almost missed our flight out of New York. We went to the airport in Frankfurt. It seemed like I walked a mile through the airport before I got to where my husband was. I was carrying two diaper bags full, one tote bag, and a twenty-five-pound little boy. It was different. We first stayed at his buddy's apartment, then in a hotel. After being there a month, they took us out to show us an apartment. The army had rented two high-rise apartment buildings connected by a parking garage. We were on the 14th floor—fifteen floors up from the parking garage. When I walked into the apartment from the wide hallway that was twelve feet wide, I could see to the other side of the apartment. I saw the balcony and the sky. I got so dizzy, especially as I walked toward the balcony. I said, "I can't live here." The person showing the apartment said, "I don't know when another one will open up. If you miss this one, it could be a while." I was tired of the hotel, so I prayed and said, "Lord, if this is where we are to live, You have got to help me." He did. By the end of the second day, I was fine. We had no car. We got a ride from a friend to go get our belongings from the hotel and some things we borrowed from the post lending closet. The things that we had shipped had not yet arrived. The first week was rough. We took the bus into the post. No bus on Sunday—no church. By Tuesday morning, I was crying. I said, "Lord, you can't bring me here like this—no car, no church, no family or friends. You've got to help me." I went to the laundry room down in the basement and met a lady named Jean (you could see Jesus coming out of the pores of her skin). She said, "Come with me to Bible study in the morning. You will love it, and we have a wonderful babysitter. I take my daughter there." I went and met so many wonderful ladies there. They had a sign in the laundry room for a non-denominational women's Bible study, but I needed to know at least one face. I was so shy then, and I didn't know the Lord as well as I should have at that time. Connie was the lady of the house. She and her husband Norm had four wonderful children—two boys and two girls. They babysat for me. Connie and Norm were Nazarenes. They worked tirelessly for the Lord and never met a stranger. Their home was Grand Central. Norm always had coffee going, and Connie had a teapot going. Norm and the kids built model airplanes two to three feet long, attached them to guide wires, and flew them. Norm would invite guys home to eat dinner. He would get them in the other half of their big dining room after dinner and get them talking about the planes, and the next thing you knew, he was talking to them about Jesus. Lots of people were led to Jesus in that apartment. One night I was down there with Connie, and another lady had come over. Her husband had guard duty that night. Connie and Norm's kids had the kids in their room playing. We were three ladies having tea. Norm had brought a new guy from work home for dinner. Dave's family had not got there yet to Germany. I think they had three kids, so they were waiting for housing first. Norm asked Dave if he was a Christian. He said no but that his wife was. The next thing we knew, we heard Norm leading Dave to Jesus. The other lady looked at Connie and me and said, "I need to do what he just did. Pray with me to accept Jesus." It's wonderful to be in the birthing room as people are born into the kingdom of God. Dave's family came. We were all just getting to know them well when they found out that Dave's wife had lung cancer. They removed it but said that it was a recurring type, so they were going to send them back to a hospital in the States that was more equipped. Before they left Germany, we were in our last church service together and an Air Force weatherman, Andy, who attended chapel with us, got us to pray for her. We all laid hands on them and prayed. God told Andy to tell her that her cancer would never come back. She was healed. I met her two years later, stateside, on another army post. She had just come from the doctor, and he told her to get out of there and quit wasting his time. Eleven doctors checked her over when she came back stateside. Cancer had never been found again. I also met a Spanish lady that our Bible study in Germany had ministered to. She was not a Christian. She had three children. She had hurt her back and was down for three weeks. We took meals, groceries, and did laundry, but she would never come to Bible study. If we saw her anywhere, we invited her. We moved two years later back stateside. While picking my kids up at the post nursery, I met the sweet, beautiful Spanish lady again. I can't remember her name, but she had a small baby. She was not supposed to have any more children. Her tubes have been tied. She was saved and leading a Bible study of fifty women. She invited me, and I went. She would come to visit me some. That Christmas morning, she called me. Her baby had died. She had been born without a spleen, and it hadn't been detected. Her baby died from a common cold. I cried with her and prayed with her. We left the army shortly after that, but I know she was surrounded by sisters in the Lord. I met so many wonderful people through the ten years my husband was in the army. God knew that I desperately needed them. I was married to an abusive alcoholic who had closed himself off from God, me, his children, and everyone. I was surrounded by good Godly people who cared for us and prayed for us. Connie and Norm were my spiritual parents. They took me under their arms for two and a half years and taught me more than anyone ever had of how to love others and walk the walk. I asked God to let me do that for others. Many young people have spent time under my arm. One little girl used to slide under my left arm every church service at the altar. I would go pray for my lost loved ones and sick loved ones. Every service, she came under that arm praying for her family too. She had a grandmother that had brought her until she was unable, and then I started bringing her to church. She took my place in the youth group as a leader when I left. Everywhere I work, God plants young people with me. Nowadays, most of them need watering with faith. They know Him but not the relationship and walk. It's an honor to have an opportunity to share Jesus and His love and word. I thank God for the people who sowed into my life.

"Being confident of this very thing, that he which hath begun a good work in you will perform it until the day of Jesus Christ" (Philippians 1:6 KJV).

"And my God will meet all your needs according to the riches of his glory in Christ Jesus" (Philippians 4:19 NIV).

To Connie and Norm:

"Whoever pursues righteousness and love finds life, prosperity and honor" (Proverbs 21:21 NIV).

"Blessed are the pure in heart, for they will see God" (Matthew 5:8 NIV).

NATHAN'S ILLNESS
AND HEALING

During our first tour of Germany with the army, I was sitting at home one day holding our two-year-old son on my lap, and I looked down and saw that he had what appeared to be drops of blood on his arms under his skin. I took him to my friend's house, who had four children. She said it looked like he had gotten pricked by a nettle bush. I told her he had not been around anything like that. She told me to just watch it for a few days because it wasn't itching, and it would probably go away. It didn't go away, so I took him by bus to the medical clinic near our home. The doctor looked at it and was concerned. They could only do minimal blood work there at the clinic. He told me to call my husband at work, tell him to get there immediately, and that we had to take him to the hospital. We took him to the hospital, and they ran blood work. They were very concerned, but they didn't know what was wrong. They told us to go back to the clinic the next day. They sent us to the hospital five days that week to check his blood work and see if there were any changes. His doctor told me that he took his medical records home with him at night and searched his medical books at night, trying to find what was wrong. One of the lab technicians who drew his blood also told me that he searched medical books at night trying to find out what was wrong with our son. One day they told me that his spleen was enlarged and might have to be removed. I asked them if he had leukemia, and they said no but that it was something with the blood. They told us if he had any changes, not to take him to the clinic but to take him straight to the hospital.

One night in the middle of the night, he woke up, doubled over screaming with his stomach. This child had never woken up during the night since he was weaned. I woke up my husband and said, "We have to take him to the hospital now." He told me that the car was on empty. Nothing was open, but the restaurants that served alcohol. He said, "There won't even be a gas station open on the interstate." I said, "You drive, and I will pray, and we will get there." He was planning to get gas on the way to work in the morning. He said, "There won't be any gas stations open now." It was 1980 in Germany. The sidewalks rolled up by 6 p.m. We drove an hour to the hospital and an hour home, and then he drove to the gas station the next morning on an empty tank. When we got to the hospital, Nathan had calmed down by then, and they couldn't find anything different or wrong with him, but my faith grew from that experience. Father God came through for us. That empty tank got us to the hospital and back—one hour each way and got him to the gas station the next morning.

During that week, on a Thursday, I gave him back to God when I put him down for a nap. I said, "God, my hope and my prayer is that You will heal my son, but if you don't, if that's not Your plan, please don't let him suffer. I'm going to love You and serve You until the day I die regardless. If You choose to take him, I will thank You always for the two years that I've had him." I took him to Bible study that night and asked them to lay hands on him and pray for his healing. That wasn't something they normally did, but they did it, and God answered. He turned forty-two years old this year. The blood spots under his skin went away, and I never took him back to the doctor because they never found out what it was. We returned to the States a year and a half later. We were in our home town, and on the news one night, there was a story about a seven-year-old little girl who walked into the emergency room and dropped dead. She had bruising on her skin. They thought she was an abuse case. They sent her body to the crime lab, and it was a rare blood disease that was so rare they normally don't find it until the child is dead. It usually occurs between the ages of two and six. This little girl was seven, so they didn't suspect it. It had a big long name that I don't remember, but I realized that had to be what God had healed my son of.

When my son's daughter was two, she developed a rash and got sick. He called me worried and wondered if it was the same thing he had when he was two. I said to him, "We'll pray, and the same God that healed you can heal her." Hers turned out to be an allergic reaction to a toy that she was chewing on. I thank God for my miracle, who now is the father of seven. God is good. My God heard the cry of my heart and answered. I will sing and proclaim the goodness of my God.

> These things I have written to you who
> believe in the name of the Son of God,
> so that you may know that you have eter-
> nal life. This is the confidence which we
> have before Him, that, if we ask anything

according to His will, He hears us. And if we know that He hears us in whatever we ask, we know that we have the requests which we have asked from Him.

1 John 5:13-15 (NASB)

BIRTHING TERI

Living in Mannheim, Germany, in 1980 with my army husband, we had gotten through the ordeal of our two-year-old son almost dying. Then in July of that year, we were also expecting another baby. She was a month and three days past her due date, and the doctor had been telling me for at least six weeks, "You won't be back next week. You will have this baby before then." Because of complications when my son was born, they would not induce labor. I woke up at 4:10 that morning to go to the restroom, and when I stood up, my water broke. I had a pain that wrapped around my stomach and back that seemed to last for about ten minutes. Silly me, I went and took a shower, put on makeup, and then woke up my husband and my mom, who had flown over for a visit. My little mama, who could not read or write, got on an airplane and flew to Germany. She was a brave soul (my daughter who was born that morning, has her faith and spirit of adventure). My husband went to get the sitter for our son. My friend Connie came and was concerned because my pains were lasting so long. We got down to the parking garage, and I was standing at the back of our Volkswagen bug when I felt an immense pain and her head delivered. I screamed. My husband said, "What are we going to do?" I said, "Have a baby right here." I had a sheet on my arm. I yelled to a friend coming through the parking garage to call an ambulance. I told my husband to go back up to our apartment and get more sheets. My mom spread the sheet out, and I delivered her with two more pains. My mom wrapped her in the bottom of the sheet and laid her on my stomach. My friend Connie sent her teenage daughter to watch our son, and then Connie went to her apartment to grab a comforter to put over us. It was fifty degrees outside.

We kept waiting on the army ambulance. It never came. In forty-five minutes, the MP came and threw his raincoat over us and called a German ambulance. In five minutes, they were loading us up in a warm ambulance. They cut her umbilical cord. By this time, she was already fifty minutes old. They wrapped her in a sheet and put her in my arms, and headed to the hospital. I said several times, "US Army hospital, Heidelberg." I could only speak English. I couldn't speak German. The young attendant, who looked like he was fifteen, couldn't speak or understand English. He was concerned that I was losing too much blood. He kept looking at me and pulling back the sheet. I would smile at him to try to tell him I was okay. I heard sirens. The ambulance stopped, and I thought that there was no way we were at the hospital yet. It was an hour's drive. I saw a helicopter landing behind us. We were on the Autobahn with a police escort. They had stopped in the middle of the Autobahn, and a doctor came on board. Then they went back to the helicopter and brought us a big comforter and covered us. The doctor could speak English. I was so tired, but he would not let me close my eyes. He asked me all kinds of questions to keep me awake and talking, but he never touched me. When we arrived at the hospital, she was two hours old. When they opened the back of the ambulance, I saw my mom and my husband looking terrified. They were sure one of us had passed away.

Everyone was just glad we were okay. We later found out the ambulance never came because the ambulance driver was not familiar with our neighborhood. There were two high risers of Americans in a German community, and there were a lot of crooks and turns to get out there, and it was dark. They fired him for refusing to come, but they had no driver to take his place. Forty-five minutes later was when the MP arrived to see if I was still there. I'm so thankful my God was there, angels, my praying mom, and our Godly friends Connie and Norm (my spiritual parents). Lots of prayers went up for us, and our Father answered. The pediatrician came to talk to me as soon as he looked her over, and he told me that he had never seen a baby born outside of the hospital come in in that good of condition. I told him that that baby was well covered in prayer. We had no complications other than my high blood pressure. It was high enough that I passed out when they let me up the first time. A US Army officer came and talked to me as soon as I was settled in my room and apologized for the fact that I didn't get an army ambulance when I needed one. He assured me that the man had been removed from the job, that everyone was glad we were okay, and if we needed anything to let them know.

> O God, listen to my cry! Hear my prayer!
> From the ends of the earth, I cry to you
> for help when my heart is overwhelmed.
> Lead me to the towering rock of safety,
> for you are my safe refuge, a fortress
> where my enemies cannot reach me. Let
> me live forever in your sanctuary, safe
> beneath the shelter of your wings!
> Psalm 61:1-4 (NLT)

NO ELEVATOR

Teri's first trip to church was when she was ten days old. My mom was still visiting with us. She had an enlarged heart, asthma, and a very bad ankle. We went to church, and all was well until we arrived back at our apartment building and realized that both elevators were out. Some teenagers had shot the windows out of both elevators with BB guns. We were in the parking garage, and our apartment was fifteen floors up (thirty flights of stairs). The doctor had told my mother to stay away from stairs. My husband carried our son, who was two years old, I carried the baby, and my mom carried the diaper bag. I was worried to death about my mom. She was worried about me. We all, by the grace of God, made it fine. We were praying for each other, and our God took care of each of us. That's why they call Him amazing. He gives strength to His people.

> "Even youths grow tired and weary, and young men stumble and fall; but those who hope in the Lord will renew their strength. They will soar on wings like eagles; they will run and not grow weary, they will walk and not be faint" (Isaiah 40:30-31 NIV).

SACRIFICIAL LOVE

We were coming up to the end of our tour of Germany in 1981. We were hoping to get in on the Christmas drop. No luck. We went home in January. When we went to my mom's, it was a weekday, and to my joy and surprise, all my brothers and sisters were there. My mom had made her traditional Christmas dinner with all the trimmings, and they had cut and decorated a fresh tree. It was wonderful. I was recently thinking back on that day and realized what a sacrifice they each had made for me. I know none of them could afford to lose a day's pay—especially right after Christmas. I was so excited about being home and enjoying Christmas dinner with my family and showing off my beautiful children. I'm sure I didn't properly thank them for their sacrificial gift. I did feel very loved that day. I have a wonderful family, many of whom are with Jesus now. I love you all, and I thank God for each of you. I am loved and blessed. My life has been changed and enriched by each of you. Thank you.

> "Three things will last forever—faith, hope and love—and the greatest of these is love" (1 Corinthians 13:13 NLT).

PRAYING FOR YOUR CHILDREN'S MATES

In 1981, my son was almost four, and my daughter was one and a half. One Sunday morning at the military chapel in Mannheim, Germany, the chaplain talked to us about praying for our children's mates. He had two young daughters. He said, "While your children are yet babies, ask God to raise up a mate for your child, one that He picks out and that if your child ever starts to stray, the mate will pull them back and that they will be good for each other all the days of their lives." I watched God answer those prayers. I am the grandmother of nine now. I met my daughter-in-law and her family when she was a toddler. We went to church together for a while, then we changed churches, and in a year or so, they started coming to that church too. My daughter-in-law is four years younger than my son. I would never have thought of her as my daughter-in-law. She was just a little girl to me, who always asked me for chewing gum and would say, "I love you." I would always say, "You only love me because I have chewing gum." I have a drawing on my bedroom wall that she made for me at about age eleven with the cross, crown of thorns, and scarlet scarf. She wrote on there, "I love you. You mean a lot to me." I taught her in Sunday school, children's church, AWANA, and youth group, never dreaming that she would be my daughter-in-law one day. They celebrated twenty years of marriage this year. I still stand amazed.

When my daughter was in college, I was concerned that she was dating the wrong people. I prayed and asked God to put a dividing line between her and anyone that she didn't need to be with. She came home from college and told me that she was going to transfer to another college. It was at the second college that she found her freedom of worship. She worked at Walmart while in college a new guy started working there. He had been frustrated that he had not found a good girl to date and his godfather told him that maybe God wanted him to work on his relationship with Him first. They had their first date three months after working together. The first time I met him, he had come over for dinner. He reached and got both of our hands and prayed the blessing over the food, and I thought, *This could be the one.* About a month later, my daughter asked me what I thought about him, and she said, "He feels like the other half of me that's always been missing." I knew he was the one. Eighteen years later, I am still convinced.

> "Call to Me, and I will answer you, and show you great and mighty things, which you do not know" (Jeremiah 33:3 NASB).

FROM GOD'S HAND TO MINE AND TO MY SISTER IN NEED

After returning to Georgia from our first tour of Germany, we were stationed in Fort Benning, Georgia. I met a lady named Margie in our subdivision. We went to chapel together, and she invited me to a ladies' Bible study. We went together every week. One week she called me and said she couldn't go and that I needed to find another ride. I got a ride to Bible study, and when they asked for prayer requests, I told them that my husband's check had not arrived, and I asked them to pray that it would arrive in a few days. I told them that there was nothing that we needed except for it to show up in a few days because it was supposed to have arrived already. After Bible study, someone came up to me and gave me fifteen dollars. I told her that we didn't need it, that we had everything we needed. She insisted that God had told her to give it to me and that I had to take it whether I needed it or not. One of the ladies dropped me back home after Bible study, and within minutes, my friend Margie showed up. She said, "Vickie, my husband hasn't sent me any money yet." He had been moved ahead of them to Alaska. She said, "I didn't come to Bible study because I didn't have gas this morning. I need to borrow fifteen dollars, and I will pay you back when I get money from my husband." I handed her the fifteen dollars and said, "This is a gift sent to you from God, and you don't have to pay it back." I told her that it wasn't my money. It was hers from the beginning. God had sent it to her.

> "But my God shall supply all your need
> according to His riches in glory by Christ
> Jesus" (Philippians 4:19 KJV).

OUT OF THE MOUTH
OF A CHILD

My husband got out of the army in 1983 and went back in 1984. During that time, we lived in Georgia. He took a second shift job. His drinking was bad at that point. I had gotten him a dark brown recliner after we had returned to the States, and the kids always saw him sitting there drinking or passed out. If he was home, he spent most of his time in that recliner. He didn't go to church with us at that time, but we were very active in the church. We were driving home from church one Sunday, and my six-year-old son said, "Mama, why does daddy not go to church with us? Does he love that old black chair more than he does God?" I was shocked. I didn't know what to say, but it amazed me that that was what he saw. I told him daddy was tired and going through a rough time. He had seen too many of his dad's rough times. His dad did occasionally go throughout the years, but he had commitment issues in his life always. I thank God that my son accepted Jesus at the age of nine and my daughter at the age of seven and that they and my grandchildren walk before God in faithfulness. They don't have commitment issues. They are very committed to their God, their spouses, and their children. I am blessed.

"Start children off on the way they should go, and even when they are old they will not turn from it" (Proverbs 22:6 NIV).

HELD

While in Germany on our second tour with my military husband, he was going through a lot of stress. He was never a people person but more of a loner. If his day went bad at work, when he came home, he took it out on me. He had drunk for a couple of hours by the time dinner was over. I had the kids in bed, usually before he was ready to fight. I had started praying for the Lord to help me not to argue with him and to help me stay quiet, so God taught me to sing. When you are praising God through word or song, you don't get angry. Your mind stays on Him. One night he tried to start an argument. I had just put the children to bed, so I decided to clean the table and do the dishes. No dishwasher—that was me. He was trying hard to pick a fight. I was washing dishes quietly singing "Victory in Jesus," and he yelled, "Shut up that singing!" He couldn't hear me, but since I was not arguing back, he knew it was because I was singing. I kept singing quietly. He started telling me that I sang terribly. I ignored him and kept quietly singing. He came into the kitchen, grabbed a sharp knife out of the dish drainer, and pulled my head back with the knife to my throat. I didn't try to move or make a sound. He turned me loose in a minute and threw the knife on the floor as he walked away. I reached down, picked up the knife, washed it, and resumed singing quietly. He couldn't hear me, but he knew since I wasn't upset that I had to be singing. He came back and grabbed the faucet of the sink and bent it all out of shape. I didn't move or speak. I just kept singing. The demon on him retreated, and the rest of the night was quiet.

> Shout joyfully to the Lord, all the earth.
> Serve the Lord with gladness and delight;
> Come before His presence with joyful singing.
> Know and fully recognize with gratitude that the Lord Himself is God;
> It is He who has made us, not we ourselves [and we are His].
> We are His people and the sheep of His pasture.
> Enter His gates with a song of thanksgiving And His courts with praise.
> Be thankful to Him, bless and praise His name. For the Lord is good;
> His mercy and lovingkindness are everlasting, His faithfulness [endures] to all generations.
> Psalm 100 (AMP)

> I will lift up my eyes to the hills [of Jerusalem]—From where shall my help come?
> My help comes from the Lord, Who made heaven and earth. He will not allow your foot to slip;
> He who keeps you will not slumber.
> Psalm 121:1-3 (ESV)

"The Lord has heard my supplication [my plea for grace]; The Lord receives my prayer" (Psalm 6:9 NASB).

SLEEPING IN PEACE AND SAFETY

One night in Germany, my husband was agitated over a bad workday, drinking too much and wanting to fight. I was exhausted. It had been a long day with a baby and a toddler (who was potty training). He kept wanting to fight. I remember going to bed to try to avoid being beaten. He came into the room and threw things at me. Then he returned and spat on me. I was so exhausted but afraid to sleep, not knowing what was coming next. I prayed and said, "God, can I just crawl up in Your lap and rest until the morning?" I got an image in my mind of a big throne with a big God sitting on it. It was all white, and he was dressed in white. I looked like a two-year-old in my mind compared to His size. I crawled up in His lap, and He put his arms around me, and I slept and woke to a better day.

> "In peace I will lie down and sleep, for
> you alone, Lord, make me dwell in safety"
> (Psalm 4:8 NIV).

One night in one of the battles, he came toward me, telling me that he was going to kill me and all the ways he was going to do it. I was standing there in terror. At our ladies' Bible study, we sang scriptures, and one began to play in my head, "The steadfast love of the Lord never ceases. His mercies, they never come to an end. They are new every morning" (Lamentations 3:22-23 ESV). I knew I would see another morning. Our Father does not want us to live this way. If you are in an abusive relationship, please leave. It doesn't get better, no matter how many promises they make.

> "In the same way, the Spirit helps us in our weakness. We do not know what we ought to pray for, but the Spirit intercedes for us through wordless groans" (Romans 8:26 NIV).

HEARING GOD

When my husband and I were in Germany for the second tour of his army career, I met a lady—she said just to call her Dede. She was from Thailand. She had three children, and we became very good friends. We talked about God a lot. She was telling me a story one day and said she had heard God speak. Once for sure. One day, when her first child was a baby, she had sat him on the table in a carry-all seat. She was doing dishes and had her back turned to him. She said he wasn't moving around much yet, so she had not fastened him in. She said she heard a loud voice say, "Turn around!" but she knew that she was alone. She turned around just in time to catch her son as he flipped out of the carry-all seat. She said, "I know it was God who spoke to me and saved my baby's life."

> "Now to Him who is able to keep you from stumbling, and to make you stand in the presence of His glory blameless with great joy, to the only God our Savior, through Jesus Christ our Lord, be glory, majesty, dominion, and authority, before all time and now and forever. Amen" (Jude 1:24-25 NASB).

COVERED AND KEPT

My friend Paula's husband had a van. They had three children. We were all in Germany and went to chapel together. He would go out to his van when possible at work and pray over all kinds of situations. It was his prayer closet. He would pray to and from work in his van. One night he was hit head-on by a drunk driver. There were four adult people in the car—three of which lost one or both of their legs because of the severity of the crash. Daryl was not hurt, even though it totaled his van. God protected him. He was a mighty man of God, married to a mighty woman of God. They were both prayer warriors. Paula and our friend Gwen covered me in prayer daily. Thanks to all those who prayed for me day and night. It is why I am here alive today to tell the stories of God's amazing grace and mercy.

> "But blessed are those who trust in the LORD and have made the LORD their hope and confidence" (Jeremiah 17:7 NLT).

> "I keep my eyes always on the LORD. With him at my right hand, I will not be shaken" (Psalm 16:8 NIV).

"For we are God's handiwork, created in Christ Jesus to do good works, which God prepared in advance for us to do" (Ephesians 2:10 NIV).

WINTERTIME MID-1980S

I was married to a man who was fighting a lot of demons in his life. He had been through a lot of trauma from age one when his dad died of a brain tumor. He was molested as a child and was threatened, so he wouldn't tell. He had friends as a teenager who began to give him alcohol and marijuana. It soothed the wounds, so he became addicted. He had given his heart to Jesus at the age of eleven and was baptized, but as he found this group of friends, he went to church less and less. His mom let him quit church at age fifteen or sixteen, which was a big mistake (if they are still under your roof, make them go. I'm thankful I never had to make my children go. They always loved church). When I met him, he was twenty-one. I was twenty-four and had already had a failed marriage and no children. He told me that he had done a lot of drinking and pot and some other drugs but that he was done with that life, and he was ready to settle down and have a family. I was a new Christian. He had gotten saved but did not have a relationship. He would relapse a day here and there. I didn't realize it would become permanent. He had told me he was going into the army. We married in November 1976. He left for boot camp in January of 1977. After a couple of years, the relapses became more frequent as the job's stress got worse. I didn't realize that he had always had bad work ethics and had never held a job for very long. I met him at

79

work. That was probably the longest job he ever kept—about a year. He was in the army for ten years, but he hated it. He lost his career over drinking. He was a tormented man. I can see it now, but when you are a beaten and abused wife, all you see is your pain and struggle. He really needed help but always refused it. The army put him through rehab many, many times, but he would never talk to them. (He never told me why he was so angry until after twelve years of marriage and two divorces.) I would ask him what was inside him to make him so angry. He would not say. He drank every day, and he would get so violent. I was the one there, so I was his punching bag. He had left for his second tour of Germany. I was left with the kids and bills, and he was sending no support. I wasn't sure I ever wanted him to come home or for me to go with him. I was working. It was never enough. Our children were four and six. I slept very little. I began to have feelings for someone that I worked with and was trying to fight it. It was getting strong. It had started with me witnessing to him, but the devil knew that I was lonely and jumped on that. I quit the job to get away from the temptation. I got another job. I had worked in carpet mills for most of my life. All of a sudden, I was allergic to the yarn—never before, but now I was. They let me go because of it. I was so depressed that I was having bad headaches. I didn't know what to do. My husband was not communicating or sending any help. God made me go back to the job that I had before, and He gave me the strength to get through. I came close to falling, but God sent help. I went to my pastor and his wife and told them what I was going through. They prayed for me and assured me that God would give me the strength to stand. I started to divorce my husband, and I thought of dating the other man, but I asked God for wisdom, and I asked Him to answer me through three people within the body of believers that did not know my situation. Within 24 hours, I got a call from my spiritual mom, who was in Texas. I was in Georgia, and I had not seen her in two and a half years, but we would talk at least once a year. She said, "What's going on? God told me to call you." I told her the situation, and she told me not to go there, that it would only cause more pain. I knew she was right. She asked me if I wanted to talk to her husband, and I said yes. She put him on the phone, and he gave me the same advice, and the two of them encouraged me in the faith. He asked me if I would like their pastor to call me, and I said yes. He encouraged me and gave me the same counsel. I had the three people I had asked for. It wasn't what I wanted to hear at the time, but I knew it was right, and I listened. Our God is faithful.

> Therefore, I urge you, brothers and sisters, in view of God's mercy, to offer your bodies as a living sacrifice, holy and pleasing to God—this is your true and proper worship. Do not conform to the pattern of this world, but be transformed by the renewing of your mind. Then you will be able to test and approve what God's will is—his good, pleasing and perfect will.
>
> Romans 12:1-2 (NIV)

> "Create in me a pure heart, O God, and renew a steadfast spirit within me" (Psalm 51:10 NIV).

> "Watch and pray so that you will not fall into temptation. The spirit is willing, but the flesh is weak" (Matthew 26:41 NIV).

GOD'S FAITHFULNESS

My husband was in the army in the 1970s and 1980s. We had two tours in Germany. Our second tour was from 1983-1986. At some point during that tour, I had to go on the bus from the army post we lived on to where the hospital was. It was an hour-long trip. Coming back on the bus, I sat with a young mother from India. When she was in England going to school, she met an American soldier and married him. We all ended up on the army post together in Germany. I met her on the bus ride back to post, and as we talked, she told me she was a Christian, and since I can't talk without talking about Jesus, she knew that I was too. She shared with me that she was about to have surgery and that she had prayed for someone she could trust to watch her two little boys. Her husband, like mine, drank too much, and she was afraid to leave her little boys with him overnight alone, so she chose to have the surgery while he was gone on field duties. She didn't tell him she was going to have surgery because he would have wanted to come home, and with his heavy drinking, she was afraid he would have a drinking party with a bunch of the guys. On the bus ride that day, she said to me, "I think you are the one that God has sent. Will you watch my two little boys?" and I did. I guess this just shows how God answers our prayers through the body of believers who are often strangers. She had a need, and I had the availability.

Each day we never know where God's direction will lead and who we might meet along the way.

> "Therefore my heart is glad and my tongue rejoices; my body also will rest secure" (Psalm 16:9 NIV).

> "And this is the confidence that we have in him, that, if we ask any thing according to his will, he heareth us" (1 John 5:14 KJV).

FINDING MONEY

My husband was away on field duties one time while we were stationed in Germany, and I thought that I had everything I needed until he came home, but one day we ran out of milk and bread, and I was out of money. I said to God, "These children need milk and bread. I need two dollars." This was in the 1980s, and you could get a loaf of bread for one dollar and a half-gallon of milk for one dollar. My husband was going to be home in two days. I walked down to the school to meet the kids and walk them home. As we walked that same sidewalk back to our apartment, my son said, "Look, mom!" In the grass beside the sidewalk, there were three one-dollar bills. I said to my son, "I just asked God for two dollars, and I just walked this sidewalk going to the school and didn't see it." So we turned around and went to the commissary, which was by the school. We got milk and bread, and I told him that he could choose what he wanted to spend the other dollar on since he found the money. He chose cookies, and we all enjoyed them. Our God is faithful, even in the little things.

> "And if we know that he hears us, whatsoever we ask, we know that we have the petitions that we desired of him" (1 John 5:15 KJV).

CALLED OUT

In 1985, I went to a revival at my mom's church during my visit home with my family. There was a pastor preaching that I had never heard before, and I didn't know him. At the end of the service, when everyone stood for prayer, the pastor called me up and told me that God told him to pray for me for strength. He said, "You are about to go through a battle, and God says you are going to need a lot of people covering you. Stay close to Him and His people, or you will not make it through." When I went back to Germany, I went through several nights that I didn't think I would see another morning. The very first night back, my husband almost killed another person and me. When we go through a fiery battle, we have to remember He is in the fire with us. Just as He was with the three Hebrew boys in the book of Daniel, and theirs was a real fire. Ours is a fiery battle with the enemy of our soul, but just the same as He delivered them, He will deliver us when we call on His name.

> So Shadrach, Meshach, and Abednego, securely tied, fell into the roaring flames.
> But suddenly, Nebuchadnezzar jumped up in amazement and exclaimed to his advisers, "Didn't we tie up three men and throw them into the furnace?"

"Yes, Your Majesty, we certainly did," they replied.

"Look!" Nebuchadnezzar shouted. "I see four men, unbound, walking around in the fire unharmed! And the fourth looks like a god!"

Then Nebuchadnezzar came as close as he could to the door of the flaming furnace and shouted: "Shadrach, Meshach, and Abednego, servants of the Most High God, come out! Come here!"

So Shadrach, Meshach, and Abednego stepped out of the fire. Then the high officers, officials, governors, and advisers crowded around them and saw that the fire had not touched them. Not a hair on their heads was singed, and their clothing was not scorched. They didn't even smell of smoke!

Then Nebuchadnezzar said, "Praise to the God of Shadrach, Meshach, and Abednego!" He sent his angel to rescue his servants who trusted in him. They defied the king's command and were willing to die rather than serve or worship any god except their own God. Daniel 3:23–28 NLT

But you, Lord, are a shield around me, my glory, the One who lifts my head high.

I call out to the Lord, and he answers me from his holy mountain. I lie down and sleep;
I wake again, because the Lord sustains me.

Psalm 3:3-5 (NIV)

In you, Lord, I have taken refuge; let me never be put to shame. In your righteousness, rescue me and deliver me; turn your ear to me and save me. Be my rock of refuge, to which I can always go; give the command to save me, for you are my rock and my fortress. Deliver me, my God, from the hand of the wicked, from the grasp of those who are evil and cruel.

Psalm 71:1-4 (NIV)

As for me, I will always have hope; I will praise you more and more. My mouth will tell of your righteous deeds, of your saving acts all day long—though I know not how to relate them all. I will come and proclaim your mighty acts, Sovereign Lord; I will proclaim your righteous deeds, yours alone. Since my youth, God, you have taught me, and to this day I declare your marvelous deeds. Even when I am old and gray, do not forsake me, my God, till I declare your power to the next generation, your mighty acts to all who are to come. Your righteousness, God,

reaches to the heavens, you who have done great things. Who is like you, God?
Psalm 71:14-19 (NIV)

"Sovereign Lord, my strong deliverer, you shield my head in the day of battle" (Psalm 140:7 NIV).

WHEN WE SING PRAISES, STRONGHOLDS ARE BROKEN

In the summer of 1985, while we were in Germany, my army husband was going for field maneuvers for two or three weeks, so the children and I came home to the US for a visit. A few days later, a plane was hijacked, and many passengers were on board. One man was killed. The hostages were taken to another country and hid and held captive. Seven days before their release, we had started a revival at my mother's little country church where I was saved eight or nine years earlier. That Sunday night, I asked the church to pray for the hostages to be released safely and for their families and for the family of the man who was killed. The piano player began to play "When the Saints Go Marching In." It lifted everyone's spirits. God spoke to me and said, "If you will get up and march around this church seven times tonight and every night of this revival to this song, I will tear down the walls that are holding the captives and set them free—just like I took down the walls of Jericho." I was afraid and didn't get up. One of the saints of the church, mother Thomason, got up and started around the church. When she passed me, I fell in line behind her, and I started pulling people off the pews to join in. The piano player kept playing "When the Saints Go Marching In," and I told them what God had said. We did it every night, and as we met for church the next Sunday morning, the hostages were on their way home. Praise God. He is still tearing down walls. I see a lot of it in prison ministry.

> "By faith the walls of Jericho fell, after the army had marched around them for seven days" (Hebrews 11:30 NIV).

> "Now to him who is able to do immeasurably more than all we ask or imagine, according to his power that is at work within us" (Ephesians 3:20 NIV).

LADIES RETREAT IN MUNICH—MY FATHER, MY FATHER, MY FATHER

In the 1980s, when my husband was stationed in Heilbronn, Germany, the chapel arranged for several of the ladies in our chapel to go to a huge ladies retreat in Munich. We took the train there and roomed together. They had sent ladies from all over Europe and mixed us up in Bible study groups. On the first day of the retreat, I met a lady and connected with her. She had a lot more wisdom in God than I did, and I wanted it. She made me hungry for God. During the break that morning, she told me that at lunchtime, there would be a room unlocked in the hotel for people to go in and pray if they wanted to instead of going to lunch. I had been saved at that point for nine or ten years, but I didn't think that God loved me, only Jesus. I saw them as two separate people. I went up to that room and found me a spot and got on my knees beside a bed, and I said, "God, whatever you have for me, I want it." I came to myself lying flat on my back, looking up into a bright light, and I was saying, "My Father, my Father, my Father." For the first time in my life, I felt God's love for me and understood that He loved me. I was one of those people who knew Jesus loved everybody, but I thought

God was judgmental and mean and was watching and waiting to punish me. My earthly father was mean, and at eleven years old, he basically sold me to a man for a six-pack of beer. I knew Jesus loved me, but now I know a Father who loves me. He's a good, good Father.

> "For there are three that bear witness in heaven: the Father, the Word, and the Holy Spirit; and these three are one" (1 John 5:7 NKJV).

A Hug to Remember

On our second tour of Germany at the Heilbronn chapel, I met many wonderful women of God. My friend Paula really pulled me in. She was always inviting me over. She was a prayer warrior and a prayer partner. Paula was a hugger and hugged everybody. She said, "My husband can't give me enough hugs, so I have to have hugs from everybody." At chapel one day, she introduced me to a lady named Jo. A week or so later I went to Paula's and Jo was there. When I walked in, they were in the kitchen, and Paula immediately hugged me as always, so then I turned, and I hugged Jo. With her arms to her side, she was stiff as a board and didn't hug me back. She immediately said, "I have to go." and she left. I looked at Paula and asked, "What just happened here?" Paula told me that Jo was abused as a child and didn't like people to touch her. I felt terrible. I went home, and I cried, and I prayed, and I said, "God, that's my sister in Christ, and I didn't mean to offend her. Help her to know that I love her, and I didn't mean to hurt her feelings." I asked Him to bind our hearts together in Him. I saw Jo a few days later. She looked at me and said, "Where's my hug?" From then on, Jo and I always greeted each other with a hug and became wonderful friends.

We both ended up going back to the States and back to Georgia. I was in North Georgia, and she was in Middle Georgia. We met halfway at Stone Mountain when they came back from Germany and had a family day together. I was divorced at that time. Our children were the same ages. They came for a visit, and then later, we found out that Jo had colon cancer. At that point, I couldn't afford to travel. She was sick and couldn't travel. She would call me in the middle of the night and then say, "I'm sorry I woke you up." I told her, "I'm your friend and your sister. You can wake me up any time." I prayed that God would always bind our hearts together. A friend gave me a house dress that snapped down the front with pockets. It was too big for me, but it fit Jo perfectly since she had gained weight. It had double hearts intertwined all over it. I went down for a visit, and I took it to Jo. I said, "No matter how far we are apart, just like these hearts, our hearts will always be intertwined." I thank God for Jo. She didn't make it through her cancer battle, but I know she is with Jesus, and I will see her again. I will never forget the first hug she ever gave me.

"A real friend sticks closer than a brother" (Proverbs 18:24 NLT).

"Dear friends, let us love one another, for love comes from God. Everyone who loves has been born of God and knows God" (1 John 4:7 NIV).

ANSWERED PRAYERS

We returned home from Germany for the last time in December of 1986, and my husband left for Kansas in January 1987. I decided not to go. I put the kids in school in Georgia and got a job, and stayed at my mother-in-law's house. She had a lot of room, and my parents didn't. I had a mole that the doctor thought was cancerous, and I was convinced, by the evil one who is always talking negatively to us, that I was going to die. I prayed and asked God to take care of my children. I had not yet learned to trust. I prayed for healing, but I said, "God, if I should have to leave my children, I need to know that they are saved and will follow me one day to heaven." I didn't know how to talk to them about it. I prayed with them but not for salvation. We were in church the next Sunday morning. We had a new pastor. It was his first Sunday. At the end of the message, my daughter said, "Mama, will you go to the altar with me?" I said, okay. I had brought these kids to the altar with me all of their lives (I couldn't leave them alone on the pew) while I would pray for their daddy to stop drinking and commit his ways to the Lord. So I said, "What's wrong?" She said, "I need to be saved." The preacher led her to Jesus. It made his day and ours. She was seven.

Three weeks later, I had to work on Sunday. I worked every other Sunday. I worked in the kitchen at the nursing home. I got up and was getting the kids ready for church when my nine-year-old son informed me, for the first time in his life, that he was not going to church. I said, "Of course you're going to church." His dad was in Kansas, and he knew that he wasn't going, so he said to me, "Dad's not going, you're not going, and I'm not going." I said, "Wrong answer, young man. You are getting in that car with your grandmother and going to church." He was mad. I said, "Son, some people have to work on Sundays. I can't tell those little people at the nursing home that they can't eat today because I want to go to church." I said, "If you fall and break a leg, you'll be happy to know that a doctor and a nurse are working today." So in the car, he went. As I was driving to work, the devil spoke in my ear and said, "He'll never go to church when he grows up because you're shoving it down his throat." Then God spoke to me in the other ear and said, "Train up a child in the way he should go, and when he is old, he will not depart from it" (Proverbs 22:6 ESV). He got saved that Sunday at church. I hated that I missed it, but when he was eleven or twelve, I got to pray a prayer of rededication with him. He told me that he needed it.

He has always had a strong faith and love for God. He said his first prayer out loud at age one and a half. He could talk as well as most three-year-olds by then. I had a couple of pictures by the table. One was a man with a bowed head with his Bible, bread and a cup. I had the same picture but with a woman. He asked me what the people in the pictures were doing, and I told him they were praying over their food. Then he bowed his head and prayed over his food. He also prayed for his friend who got hurt and got stitches when he was two. When he was two, and I was in the hospital after giving birth to my daughter, my mom was with him, and he asked her to get down on the floor and play with him. She told him she couldn't because her bad ankle hurt too bad. She said he knelt and put his hands on her ankle and prayed and then asked her if it was better and if they could play. She told me it was still hurting but that she got down and played because she wanted him to always believe in prayer. Thank you, mama (He was two, but if you have older children, you can explain that sometimes our prayers don't get answered immediately).

Nathan is forty-two as I write this, and he and his wife and children are in God's house weekly. At one point in his thirties, he got out of church for a while. He was working hard and just was getting frustrated with the politics of the church. I prayed and reminded God about what He told me the day my son got saved—if I trained him up in the Lord, he would not depart. I said, "God, he has departed Your house, and this one is on You." A few days later, my son called, and as we talked, he said, "Mom, I've been thinking about getting back in church." I said, "Praise God. That's good news." And thank you, John-Paul (our executive pastor), for praying with me during that time for my son. You are a great man of God and a great prayer warrior.

"The Lord makes firm the steps of the one who delights in him;" (Psalm 37:23 NIV).

Let the morning bring me word of your unfailing love, for I have put my trust in you. Show me the way I should go, for to you I entrust my life. Rescue me from my enemies, Lord, for I hide myself in you.

Teach me to do your will, for you are my God; may your good Spirit lead me on level ground.

Psalm 143:8-10 NIV

"For it is by grace you have been saved, through faith—and this is not from yourselves, it is the gift of God—not by works, so that no one can boast. For we are God's handiwork, created in Christ Jesus to do good works, which God prepared in advance for us to do" (Ephesians 2:8-10 NIV).

A RIDE TO REMEMBER

In 1987, my husband left the military. I was still in Georgia with the children staying with his mother. It was a difficult time. His drinking and lifestyle had gotten out of control. I left and took the kids and was going to file for divorce. After a few weeks, he talked me into coming back, and things were better. He wasn't drinking, and he had gotten a job. Then weeks later, he disappeared. We were sick with worry. After three days, we found out he was in jail in Tennessee for a DUI. I begged his mom to leave him a little while and let him dry out, but she wouldn't. He came home as if nothing had ever happened. No apologies. No job now. So we had a fight. He hurt me pretty badly. If his mom had not stopped him, I might have been a fatality. His mom and I both went to work the next day. I was in a lot of pain, but I knew I had to work, and so did his mother. The next two nights, he went partying with his friends, coming in at 4 a.m. She was worried, and so was I. Thursday night, he came in at 2 a.m. sitting in the driveway revving the engine turning the radio up wide keeping us up, but we knew better than to approach him or say anything. About 4 a.m., he came in and went to sleep in the den with his clothes, boots, and everything on the sofa. I got ready for work early and went and cranked my car. It hurt to walk or move from the beating he had given me Monday night. There was about an eighteen-inch-long piece of two-by-four laying next to my car. I took it inside. Please don't anyone else do this. Just leave. What I did was very wrong and could have had horrendous consequences. God does not want us in an abusive relationship. I went in and tied his boot strings through the Afghan on the sofa and pushed the coffee table in front, and hit him in the head with the two-by-four. It sounded like his head popped. I didn't mean to hurt him badly. I just wanted him to feel some pain and to realize I had had enough. I thought I had killed him. I ran and got in my car and headed for the interstate and for the mountain, thinking it was better for me to be dead than for my children to visit me in prison for twenty years for killing the man who had beat me for years. As I was driving grief-stricken and thinking, "How did I allow myself and my children to get to this place?" the Holy Spirit of God got in the car with me and said, "Stop this car. Do not go to that mountain." I kept driving. I could not see Him, but I could feel His tangible presence beside me. He said to me several times, "Stop this car. Do not go to the mountain." getting a little louder each time. I kept driving. Then He said to me not long before I went to turn to go up the mountain, "Stop and call. He is not dead. Stop this car and call. He is not dead." So I went to a phone and called. When his mother answered, I said, "Is he dead or alive?" She laughed and said, "He's okay. He's just got a bump on his head." I went to work and got off early and went to the lawyer's office, and filed for divorce. I called my sister to see if we could stay for a few days and went to get my kids. My mother-in-law told me they were at her daughter's house. She said, "He is drunk, and he's got a gun somewhere, and he's looking for you. Get these kids away and go hide." We stayed with my sister for two years. He was afraid of her husband. As soon as I got on my feet and bought a house, he started calling wanting to get back together. We remarried three and a half years later. After eighteen months of going to church and Godly dating, he was back to his old self in less than three months. He had serious problems. We can't fix those, only God can, and He can do it, but the one in need of help has to want it. God can work better if we are not in His way. Twenty-six years later, he still cannot deal with people. It wasn't just me. We need to get out of abusive relationships and stay out.

> For I am convinced [and continue to be convinced—beyond any doubt] that neither death, nor life, nor angels, nor principalities, nor things present and threatening, nor things to come, nor powers, nor height, nor depth, nor any other created thing, will be able to separate us from the [unlimited] love of God, which is in Christ Jesus our Lord.
>
> Romans 8:38-39 (AMP)

HID IN PLAIN SIGHT

I don't remember what year, but after our second divorce, I woke up on Monday and Tuesday night. It would feel like ice water running up my spine. I was terrified. I felt that spirit that would come over my ex-husband when he would get abusive. You could see a change in him, and I thought he was in the house. I had changed the locks when I made him leave. I got up and looked through the house. No one was there. The kids were asleep. I prayed and went back to sleep. Wednesday night after church, my baby sister called and said, "Vickie, is Terry bothering you?" I said, "No, why?" I had not heard from him in months. She said, "I had a dream. I'm afraid not to tell you." I said, "Go ahead." She said, "I dreamed I came to your house and opened the kitchen door, and you and the kids were shot dead on the kitchen floor. There was blood everywhere." I didn't tell her what had happened the last two nights. I just said, "If you are concerned, pray for us. We are all fine now." Two nights later, I had taken my daughter to his mother's after I got off work on Friday. They went every other weekend. He rarely saw them. My son didn't go. He had a ball game the next day. He had gone to his friend's house across the street and had left the kitchen door unlocked. His weight bench was in front of the living room door. I was sitting watching TV and heard the kitchen door open. I looked up, and there was my

105

ex walking through. I said hello, and he didn't look at me or speak. I knew it was best for me not to move. I said, "God, if you want me protected, You are going to have to do it." I was afraid I would never make it out of the house if I moved. I knew he was going after my son's gun. He had bought him a gun to go deer hunting. I was shocked when he did; he wasn't a gift giver. I think his nephew talked him into it. He knew it would be in my son's closet, and it was standing straight up in the corner of a half-empty white closet. We didn't have much. It was easy to see. I heard him digging through the closet. I thought of trying to run, but I felt I was supposed to sit still, and he was much faster than me and had long arms. If I had tried, I might not have made it because of the house's floor plan. I heard him go to my daughter's room and look in her closet. I thought that was odd, but I sat still. He went back to my son's room looking for the gun, and I think he looked in my room in my closet. He came walking back through. Both times he looked like he was in a demonic trance. I said, "Did you find what you were looking for?" He didn't look at me or speak. He just left. I thanked the Lord, and then I heard another car. I thought he was back. My daughter and mother-in-law came running in saying, "Are you alright?" I said yes. She asked me if he had been there, and I said, "Yes, he was looking for something but didn't find it." She said, "He told me he was coming to get that gun and kill you." I said, "I guess God changed his mind." God had to have hidden that gun from him. It was in plain sight, and so was I. If he had seen me, he would have killed me. God had to have hidden me too. I didn't realize that until later. I was telling my niece, and her husband was the one who said to me, "Didn't you realize God had to have hidden you too." That's why he never looked at me or spoke. I was hidden in the cleft of God's hand.

"I have set the Lord always before me: because he is at my right hand, I shall not be moved" (Psalm 16:8 KJV).

God, My Husband

I think that when God told Moses that His name was "I Am," He was saying, "I am whatever you need me to be." When my marriage failed after trying many, many times to sustain it, I decided that this man is not coming home here anymore. As a single mom of a ten and twelve-year-old, I decided that I did not want a step-parent over them. I realize that there are many wonderful step-parents out there, but I had not made the best decisions, and I did not want to risk harm to my children. I didn't want another man in my life. I had seen a lot of damage from step-parents in my family, so I said to God, "In Isaiah 54, You said if I was a woman forsaken that you would take me up and be my husband. I am asking you to do that. You said You would be a Father to the fatherless in Psalm 68:5. I am asking you to be a father to my children and to help me raise them to walk with You. When I knew they were in the womb, I prayed and asked You to let them come to You early as little Samuel did, and they did. I am asking you to help us walk the rest of the way." My children have grown up well, and they and their children are walking with Him now. I am a woman well blessed.

"A father of the fatherless, a defender of the widows, is God in his holy dwelling" (Psalm 68:5 NIV).

"And my God will supply all your needs according to His riches in glory in Christ Jesus. Now to our God and Father be the glory forever and ever. Amen" (Philippians 4:19-20 NASB).

Isaiah 54 (read the entire chapter)

LEARNING TO PRAY

Our pastor told this story about a little man who was sick and dying. He had come to Jesus and wanted to learn how to pray. People told him different things. Someone brought him a book on prayer, but he still felt like he didn't know how to pray. He was in the hospital, and there was a chair by his bed. Someone told him to pretend that God was sitting in the chair beside him, and they said, "Talk to God like you are talking to me. Just talk to Him." When he passed away, he was found with his body leaned over into that chair, and his arms were circling it. He had put his arms around God and put his head in His lap, and went to be with Him. Talking to God is simple. Open your heart and open your mouth and just speak. He loves you. He loves your voice. Let Him hear you. As parents, we are always so excited as our children start to get old enough to speak. We can't wait to hear if it will be *mama* or *dada* first. Just as we talk to our children and want them to talk to us, so it is with our Heavenly Father. He longs to hear our voices.

> Hear my cry, O God; Give heed to my prayer. From the end of the earth I call to You when my heart is faint; Lead me to the rock that is higher than I. For You have been a refuge for me, a tower of

strength against the enemy. Let me dwell
in Your tent forever; Let me take refuge
in the shelter of Your wings
                    Psalm 61:1-4 (NASB)

FOOT WASHING

When I was in my thirties, I got to go to a foot washing—
my first and only. My sister Mary was there—she died a few
years later. I think I only washed two sets of feet—my mother's (how precious) and my sister Mary's. I am so thankful for
that experience. Mary was the first sibling to pass. She was
only forty-two. That was very difficult, but I am thankful for
the forty-two years and thankful that I got to wash her feet.
I've washed some feet since then, but not in a foot washing.
Maybe we need to bring those back. I heard a pastor on TV
one night saying that he and one of his deacons had some
different opinions on something that they were working on
at the church and that they both had been quite stubborn in
their opinions, and it caused bad feelings. He said that God
dealt with him about it, and on Sunday morning, he asked
the deacon to come up by the pulpit and sit in a chair. He
didn't tell anyone what he was doing. He just got down in
front of the man and began to wash his feet. He had a towel
and basin prepared. With tears, he asked the man's forgiveness. Before he finished, they both were in tears. The man
then asked the pastor to allow him to wash his feet and ask
his forgiveness. The pastor looked out, and people all over
the church were down with handkerchiefs and tissues, wiping each other's shoes and asking forgiveness for wrongs—

what a meeting. I can't remember, but I hope it broke out in revival. We could use some of that right now.

> Now before the feast of the Passover, when Jesus knew that his hour was come that he should depart out of this world unto the Father, having loved his own which were in the world, he loved them unto the end. And supper being ended, the devil having now put into the heart of Judas Iscariot, Simon's son, to betray him; Jesus knowing that the Father had given all things into his hands, and that he was come from God, and went to God; He riseth from supper, and laid aside his garments; and took a towel, and girded himself. After that he poureth water into a bason, and began to wash the disciples' feet, and to wipe them with the towel wherewith he was girded. Then cometh he to Simon Peter: and Peter saith unto him, Lord, dost thou wash my feet? Jesus answered and said unto him, What I do thou knowest not now; but thou shalt know hereafter. Peter saith unto him, Thou shalt never wash my feet. Jesus answered him, If I wash thee not, thou hast no part with me. Simon Peter saith unto him, Lord, not my feet only, but also my hands and my head. Jesus saith to him, He that is washed needeth not save to wash his feet, but is clean every whit: and ye are clean, but not all. For

he knew who should betray him; therefore said he, Ye are not all clean. So after he had washed their feet, and had taken his garments, and was set down again, he said unto them, Know ye what I have done to you? Ye call me Master and Lord: and ye say well; for so I am.

John 13:1-13 (NKJV)

"A new commandment I give unto you, That ye love one another; as I have loved you, that ye also love one another. By this shall all men know that ye are my disciples, if ye have love one to another" (John 13:34-35 ASV).

GOD'S PROVISION, MAMA'S HAND

In the summer of 1995, my daughter went on a mission trip. She had wanted to go for a while. I found one, but it was very expensive. I was a single mom making minimum wage. We sold donuts, did car washes, bake sales, and the church gave her an offering. A few people in the church also donated towards the trip. We finally got all the money paid for the trip. The only thing left was her ticket from Atlanta to Miami, where the group from all over the US stayed for a few days before flying to Venezuela. I didn't know how I was going to pay for it. I thought I had a couple of more weeks. On Friday afternoon, she said, "Mom, I have to call the organizer and give her my flight info on Monday morning, so we have to get the ticket this weekend." I thought, *oh my God, where is this money going to come from.* She and I went to clean the church on Saturday—what they paid me helped pay the light bill every month. When we got home, there was a message on the answering machine. My sister Rosie had called and said, "When you get home, come up here. We have a gift for Teri from her grandmother." My mom had been in heaven for six years. We went to Rosie's. She and her husband had been looking for an important piece of paper, and all of mama's papers were stored in her pocketbooks—every birth certificate, everything she considered important. They had a small table between them, and one of them found a small drawstring bag that contained money. They looked at each other, and at the same moment, they said, "This is for Teri." It was within $5 of the amount that we needed. Isn't our God good? At that moment in my mind, I saw my mother's beautiful hand put that money in that bag, and God knew what it was for. Before she died, she had told Rosie that there was some money in a bag in one of her pocketbooks to help with her funeral. She said that her insurance was small and wouldn't be enough. They had found some money in one of her pocketbooks when she died, and so they looked no further. That mission trip changed my daughter's life. She turned fifteen on that trip, and it gave her her life's direction, and I see her walk it out every day. She started studying Spanish after that trip and is now a Spanish teacher. God is so good. He is everything we need—Father, Savior, Kinsman Redeemer, Healer, Provider, and a million other things. God the Father, God the Son, and God the Holy Spirit.

"But my God shall supply all your need according to his riches in glory by Christ Jesus" (Philippians 4:19 KJV).

ASK

As I was driving to work one payday, I was thinking about the bills that had to be paid and that I would be short of what I needed. I said, "Lord, I sure could have used another $25 on that paycheck this week." I was on my job, and within thirty minutes, my supervisor said that he was going to do my job while I went to Human Resources. I asked him if I was in trouble, and he laughed and said no. I always donate money to United Way because they help so many people. They had done a drawing at work, and when I went to Human Resources, she handed me a $25 Walmart gift card. I told her that less than an hour ago, I told God that I needed $25 more this week. She said that when we give, it comes back to us when we need it.

This week I had $60 that did not have to be anywhere. I was about to go to work, and a young struggling single mom came to mind, so I put some cookies in a container in a bag and slipped the $60 under the container, and hung the bag on her door on my way to work. As soon as I got to work, I was told to go to our department manager's office. He told me that I was getting a $350 bonus for working extra hours when needed.

"for Your Father knows what you need
before you ask him" (Matthew 6:8 NIV).

God's Amazing Works

A young married couple came to work in a carpet mill where I was working about fourteen years ago. They worked on the machine beside me. We took breaks together and shared stories of our lives. He was twenty-two, and she was twenty-six, and they had two little girls who were four and six from her first marriage. It didn't take long to figure out that their marriage was in trouble. We worked third shift, and I also worked part-time at a Christian bookstore second shift. I bought them a book with some wise pastoral counsel on marriage. It helped a lot. One night as I talked to them about Jesus on break and asked if they went to church, they shared that they had been saved but had not been in church in a while. The young man told me that he was sitting in church when he was fifteen and began to feel compelled to go forward, so he prayed and said, "God, if you want me to go up to the altar, give me a sign." He said a lady on the pew in front of him turned around and said, "God wants you up there." so he went. His wife said that their six-year-old was getting up early on Sunday mornings and asking them to take her to church. They hadn't been. I talked to them about the importance of taking children to church. I bought their six-year-old a little book at the bookstore that explained salvation on a child's level and how to ask Jesus in your heart. She read it and told her mother that she had asked Jesus in her heart and said she wanted to go to church, and so they did. A couple of months later, the mom was in the kitchen cooking and looked in the living room, and her six-year-old was on the sofa reading. She said, "Are you reading your little book again?" She said, "Yes, God told me to." She asked her teacher at school why she never told them about Jesus, and she said that as a teacher, she wasn't allowed to, that she would lose her job, but she said, "You can tell anyone you want to about Jesus." We were sitting at break one night talking about work and jobs that we had had before that one. I said, "The place I worked before here paid a lot less, but when I told them that I was leaving, they asked me to please not leave and told me that I was a good worker and they wished that I would stay, but they never offered me a raise to get me to stay." This twenty-two-year-old young man said, "God wouldn't let them." I said, "What do you mean God wouldn't let them?" He said, "God needed you here to help save our marriage and get us back in church." He saw the big picture clearly. I was missing it. Sometimes it is God's will that we leave a job or lose a job. It is often His direction in our lives, and we don't see it. He has had to push me out of my comfort zone many times. I am so thankful that He loves us and others enough to do it. I saw that couple a few years later. They were still married and in church doing well. Praise God. We ask God to use us, and sometimes He needs us in a different place. He blessed them and me.

> "But in your hearts revere Christ as Lord. Always be prepared to give an answer to everyone who asks you to give the reason for the hope that you have. But do this with gentleness and respect" (1 Peter 3:15 NIV).

"He said to them, "Go into all the world and preach the gospel to all creation" (Mark 16:15 NIV).

"Therefore, since we are surrounded by such a great cloud of witnesses, let us throw off everything that hinders and the sin that so easily entangles. And let us run with perseverance the race marked out for us" (Hebrews 12:1 NIV).

SOWING SEEDS

I worked with a lady for years who wasn't saved but knew of the Christian life. She was raised in a Christian home. She believed God answered prayers. She had a twin sister who lived in another state who had multiple sclerosis, and her health was declining fast. She would tell me that her sister was a Christian. She worried about her sister's health but didn't get to visit often. She came to me often for prayer. She said, "I can't pray for her. I'm lost, and God will answer your prayers." I told her, "The one thing that your sister wants is to know that you have given your heart to Jesus and that you are going to follow her to heaven." She would say, "I can't." I would bring her tracks and books. I bought her a Bible. I had such a burden for her salvation. I tried to tell her that her sins could be forgiven just like everyone else's, but she would not budge. I asked God to reach her and not let her be left behind. The burden was so strong that one morning I went to her house and stood on her porch, crying and begging her to ask Jesus to forgive her and come into her heart. She didn't. We worked together for several years. I left that job and went to another one. She came to work one Monday, professing she had gone to church on Sunday with her son and had received Jesus. She asked a friend of mine, who still worked there, to please tell me that she had accepted Jesus, and she knew that she was going to heaven. What wonderful news. If we sow seeds, a harvest will come. It just takes longer with some. Praise our faithful Lord.

> "Those who go out weeping, carrying seed to sow, will return with songs of joy, carrying sheaves with them" (Psalm 126:6 NIV).

A Bad Night at Work

I was on the job many years ago, and a supervisor left. We were given a new one. He had never been a supervisor before and decided to implement some major changes rather suddenly. The plant manager and mechanics were on board with him, so they announced one morning that the women operators would be required to get under the machine and work on our own machines. Many of us had no training and one lady, in particular, had problems with the mechanic who wanted to get under the machine with her. We decided to make a complaint to the office, so eight ladies showed up to the plant manager's office. We had all three shifts represented. He said that he would not see us all at once, only one at a time. I prayed and said, "Lord, don't let me get upset or rude, don't let me say one word more than I need to or one word less. Fill my mouth with the right words." I was treated with respect, and he listened to me. Some of the others were not treated with respect and listened to because many of them were argumentative. He told me that they would give us the necessary training, but we would have to start working on our machines, and if we had trouble in training, he would help us work it out. I was disappointed, but okay. I went to work that night, and as I was going to the machine that I was supposed to work on, the supervisor came to me, making sure no one was around to hear. He said, "You are going to be sorry you went to the office on me." I didn't know what to say, so I said, "Well, we will see." As I went to step up on my machine, I was a little apprehensive, and I heard the Lord say very clearly, "Many are the perils of the righteous but the Lord delivers him out of them all" (Psalm 34:19). That supervisor came to my machine three times in anger that night and then one time saying, "We can work this out." Then the next time saying, "Are we okay? Can we work together? Will you work with me?" We did just fine. I think I was there about two years after that incident.

> "The righteous cry out, and the LORD hears, And delivers them out of all their troubles. Many are the afflictions of the righteous, But the LORD delivers him out of them all" (Psalm 34:17,19 NKJV).

WORKPLACE MINISTRY

Many years ago, working in a carpet mill, I started praying that God would use me every day. He answered those prayers. One year I led three young men to Jesus, and I got the opportunity to lead the two bad girls at work back to Jesus and influence many others. Another man there eventually came to Jesus after I planted lots of seeds. Someone else was talking to him too and watered those seeds. One night, as I was witnessing to him, he said, "You make it sound so simple." I said, "It is." He said, "You explain it well." I said, "Jesus made the gospel simple enough for a child to understand it. It's people who complicate it." Praise God he got saved. Back to the bad girls. We had this tall loudmouth girl from New York come to work. She was rough around the edges. She had been through a lot and somewhere along the way had lost custody of her two daughters. She was upset about that, and I, good ol' sister goody-two-shoes, was judging her for that, thinking, "What kind of mom loses her kids?" God spoke to me and told me that He wanted me to witness to her. I said, "How God? We don't speak the same language." She cussed like a sailor, and our personalities were so different that I didn't know how to talk to her. She told me later that her mama used to say when she would hear her cuss, "Girl, do you kiss your babies with that same mouth?" I had to find a way to witness to her. Every day I would see her at the water fountain as we were getting a cup of ice water at the start of our shift. I would look her in the eye, give her my best smile, and say, "Hey, how are you today?" After about a week, she came by my machine while it was down. I was reading while we were waiting for the next order. She worked in another department that came through mine to go to the restroom or the break room. She stopped and said, "What are you reading?" I said, "It's a murder mystery." I baited her a little with the book—never telling her that it was a Christian book. I said, "I'm almost done with it if you would like to read it when I finish." She said, "Sure." So there, the friendship and ministry began. The other bad girl at the carpet mill worked in my department. The two of them hated each other. They both could be heard cursing and calling each other names. One of the supervisors often had to intervene. Soon this one started reading also. I worked part-time in a Christian bookstore, and I would bring in tracts. When no one was around or in the break room, I would sneak in there and put out tracts. I could see it from my machine. One day a beautiful young Hispanic girl from the other department came to me and said, "You're the one putting the tracts in the break room. I saw you once." She thought that it was a good thing, so she went to the bookstore and got tracts, and she said she went to the big flea market in our town on Saturday and handed out tracts because of me. I commended her and told her many people might receive Jesus as a result of what she did. I soon had a book club going in my work area. Although I lost around thirty to fifty books, if it changes lives, it is worth it. That's a small cost. One of the ladies I didn't know well asked me one day after reading four or five books, "Are these Christian books? They mention God a lot." I told her they were written by a Christian. I didn't just take Christian fiction. I had many Christian books by many good authors.

At break time, I never left my machine. It was a book ministry time. One night it was 4:45 a.m. (we worked third), and one of the bad girls came to my machine. She said, "I know during break you'll have a crowd around here, so please tell me what I need to do." She said, "I was saved when I was younger, and I've lived a bad life in recent years. Please tell me how to pray my way back to Jesus, and I will go home and do it." and she did. That same week the other bad girl came to me with the same question, almost word-for-word. I told her what to pray, and she did. Those two became best friends. Everyone in the plant found out on all three shifts and was amazed. God got a lot of glory from that. One night one of the ladies' machines was running bad, and she was getting upset, then someone said something that upset her. She was about to go after them, and her supervisor said, "Don't go back to that. Look at what God has done. You don't want to go there again." She came and told me what he said and was glad he called her on it. At that time, I lived forty-five minutes from work. The two girls would come home with me some mornings and help me can homemade soup and other things after work. Then one of them moved in with me for a while and was doing good. She was in church with me and getting her girls every other weekend. We took them to church, but in a while, she met a man who took her back down the wrong road. Then another. I haven't heard from her in thirteen years. I pray she found her way back to God. She became a grandmother right before we lost touch. I pray that helped her to see the importance of how we live. Father God still has to grab me by the shirt collar occasionally. I ask Him to when I get judgmental. I say, "Lord, just grab me by the back of the neck and straighten me out." He's a good, good Father, and He does.

I love you, girls. If I don't see you again in this life, I will see you on the other side.

> "Answer me, Lord, answer me, so these people will know that you, Lord, are God, and that you are turning their hearts back again" (1 Kings 18:37 NIV).

> Seek the Lord while he may be found; call on him while he is near.
> Let the wicked forsake their ways and the unrighteous their thoughts.
> Let them turn to the Lord, and he will have mercy on them, and to our God, for he will freely pardon.
> Isaiah 55:6-7 (NIV)

A BIG HUG FROM THE HOLY SPIRIT

We used to have a small flea market in town on Saturdays, but on Fridays, it was open to farmers to sell their produce during garden season. I worked my third shift job near there. On Fridays, the farmers would be set up very early. I had gotten off of work at 7 a.m. and stopped by to see if there were any berries for sale. There was an older gentleman passing out Bible tracts. I took one, and we were talking. I grew up hating most men. I had been through a lot of abuse from them. I had three wonderful older brothers and a younger one who had never harmed me in any way, but because they were men, I did not want to be left alone in the room with them. I rarely looked at men directly in the face or in the eyes because I felt like they misinterpreted that to mean that I wanted their attention. That day I was talking so comfortably with this gentleman, and several more came and joined the conversation. It was all about Jesus, and I talked and felt at ease. There were no women around at the time. As I walked back to my Jeep, I felt the Holy Spirit wrap His arms around me and give me a big hug. I knew He was proud of me. I had overcome a milestone in my life. I can now talk freely and look the brethren in the eye. If I'm not comfortable, there is usually an inappropriate spirit there, and I can deal with it appropriately. Life is often hard on us. We all go through many trials in our lives, but we have a Comforter, a Healer, and a Father who we can crawl up on His lap.

"Be not overcome of evil, but overcome evil with good" (Romans 12:21 KJV).

"You, dear children, are from God and have overcome them, because the one who is in you is greater than the one who is in the world" (1 John 4:4 NIV).

1–800–JESUS

When I was in need of help one night and did not have a cell phone, I called 1–800–JESUS, and my answer came. I was driving to work at 10:30 one night on a dark country road with two lanes and a ditch on both sides. Someone with bright lights was blinding me. I got close to the edge and hit a busted piece of pavement. It busted my worn tire. There was no place to pull over. I drove a quarter of a mile up to the crossroad where there was a pullover spot. All the traffic had to stop before crossing. Several people passed. No one offered assistance. I prayed and said, "God, do I stay put or walk?" I knew someone who lived a few blocks away, but it can be dangerous walking through neighborhoods in the dark, so I felt I should stay put. I had a spare tire and everything I needed except for strength. I had nerve damage in both hands, and although I knew how to change a tire, I could not do it. About fifteen minutes later, someone pulled up to the stop sign and called out, "Do you need help?" I said, "Yes, I need a flat tire changed." The voice replied, "Aunt Vickie, is that you?" After a few minutes and a big hug from a sweet, helpful nephew, I was on my way. My Father didn't just send help, he sent someone familiar, so I had no reason to fear. My nephew told me that he should have been going through there an hour and a half ago, but now he knew why he couldn't get out of the house on time. The next weekend, my daughter made sure I got a cell phone, even though I insisted I was fine without one. Jesus heard me just fine and came to my rescue. He always answers.

> "Let us then with confidence draw near to the throne of grace, that we may receive mercy and find grace to help in time of need" (Hebrews 4:16 ESV).

A WET ROAD MIRACLE

I had to drive my sister's spare car while mine was in the shop one time. It was an old, worn-out Cutlass. It had to be anointed with two quarts of oil a week, and it had slick tires. I was driving to my part-time job one Saturday afternoon, and it had just started to rain. I was behind a new Honda on the bypass with five passengers in it. The light turned red, and they stopped, but the Cutlass didn't. When I hit the back of that car, my knees went weak. I turned sick. It looked like it folded the back like an accordion. It took me a couple of minutes to get out. They were all fine. When we looked at both cars, there was not a scratch or dent on either vehicle. I know it was a miracle. I hit them hard. They all got out and said, "We're okay. Let's go." God is good.

> "Lord, you are my God; I will exalt you and praise your name, for in perfect faithfulness you have done wonderful things, things planned long ago" (Isaiah 25:1 NIV).

LET THERE BE LIGHT

I met my friend Donna when she was in her twenties. Over the years, we worked together at three different places. I always talk about the Lord. I can't help it. I wouldn't want not to do it. He is such a part of my life. Donna was raised in church, knew God, and had given her heart to Him, but she had married a man who did not walk with God. He had pulled her away. She asked for prayer always for different friends and family. You could tell she missed living close to the Lord, but I could not seem to get her to get closer. She let many things get in the way. I always told her He missed their closeness, and He was waiting for her to turn herself back to Him. She called me one day. We no longer work together, and I hadn't talked to her in a while. Life gets too busy sometimes. She said, "Vickie, I was driving down the street earlier today in broad daylight, and I began to talk to the Lord. I said, "Lord, I just need Your light to turn back on in my life," and all of the interior lights in my car came on. I said, "I guess you got your answer." Praise God. She got back in church and was walking close with Him when she passed away from lung cancer.

"In him was life, and that life was the light of all mankind" (John 1:4 NIV).

"For you were once darkness, but now you are light in the Lord. Live as children of light" (Ephesians 5:8 NIV).

"When Jesus spoke again to the people, he said, "I am the light of the world. Whoever follows me will never walk in darkness, but will have the light of life" (John 8:12 NIV).

"Blessed are those who have learned to acclaim you, who walk in the light of your presence, Lord" (Psalm 89:15 NIV).

A Motherly, Wise Cat

I worked with a man in one of the carpet mills who had a son, who was eleven years old when we worked together. When he and his wife got married, they got a cat. They loved their cat. When they found out that they were going to have a baby, everyone warned them that they should get rid of their cat because it would take the baby's breath and it would be jealous of the baby. They insisted that she was a gentle cat and that they were going to keep her. The cat loved the baby, and the baby loved her. She had never gotten into the baby's crib, but one night the dad woke up to strange sounds coming from the crib. The cat was on the baby. The baby was still asleep. All of those warnings he had heard were coming back to mind. He grabbed the cat, scolded her, and slung her down the hall. As soon as he got back in the bed, the cat was back in the crib with the baby making louder sounds. He slung the cat down the hall again, but this time he felt the baby, and he was cooking with a fever. God used the cat to get him to the baby. The cat was faithful, even after being slung down the hall. As they headed to the emergency room with the baby, he realized that the cat was warning them that the baby was not okay. Anytime that child was sick, they couldn't pry the cat away from him, even at age eleven when we worked together.

"Lord, you are my God; I will exalt you and praise your name, for in perfect faithfulness you have done wonderful things, things planned long ago" (Isaiah 25:1 NIV).

"I will sing of the Lord's great love forever; with my mouth I will make your faithfulness known through all generations" (Psalm 89:1 NIV).

A Sad Ending That Did Not Need to Be So

I worked with a man who was probably in his late 30s. In the workplace, you see and hear a lot. I had worked with his dad on another job, so we talked occasionally. I saw as he was having an affair with a woman at work. His wife and kids went to church. She was a Christian. He loved his wife but got caught up in the moment and had an affair. I saw his pain and remorse, and I knew that it was eating him up. I felt the Lord wanted me to reach out to him, so I purposely walked by his machine. The pain was all over his face. I went over to him and said, "You seem to be going through a painful time. I want you to know that I'm praying for you." A few days later, a friend and I walked by the machine, and we stopped to talk to his co-worker. She was a new Christian and on fire for the Lord. We talked about God and the revival she had gone to with my sister and a couple of friends. As we talked, his eyes never left my face. He was drinking in every word I said. When we walked away, my friend that was with me said, "Did you see his face as you were talking? It was like he was in a trance. His eyes never left your face." I said, "He needs Jesus, and he knows, but maybe he doesn't know how." The next night before work, I worked my part-time job at the Christian bookstore. My eye caught a men's study Bible, and I almost bought it for him, but I hesitated and got distracted and never got it. When I went to work that night, I saw him at the ice machine. We were both getting a cup of ice water to take to our jobs. I asked how he was and said to him, "I almost bought you a study Bible tonight. I was thinking of you at the bookstore." We went on to our jobs, and at our 5 a.m. break, I was the only one at my machine, and he came to my machine and said, "Did you say you got me a Bible?" I said, "No, I almost did. I'll get it for you if you would like." I said a few words to him about the peace and forgiveness of Jesus, and I said, "If you would ever like to ask Jesus into your heart, I would be honored to pray with you." He said that he wanted to, so we prayed, and he accepted Jesus. He was going to church and reading the Bible I got him, even at work on his breaks. He did well for a while, and then I saw another woman going after him. I tried to warn him that Satan wanted to take him down. He didn't listen. He had an affair with a very wicked woman who I think told his wife because he wouldn't leave his wife for her. His wife had a heart problem. They didn't know about it, and she died. I think from a broken heart. Jesus took her out of the continual pain of betrayal. This man had a real problem with lust. Jesus can deliver us from all things. Pornography is a serious problem that leads to lust and unfaithfulness. It's bad, and sometimes it takes fasting and prayer. Jesus told his disciples that some demons only come out with fasting and prayer (Mark 9:29). I pray that he has found his walk with Jesus. I haven't seen him in fourteen years. The spirit of lust seems to have overtaken the world, but prayer, faith, and fasting can deliver you and your loved ones.

"And he said unto them, This kind can come forth by nothing, but by prayer and fasting" (Mark 9:29 KJV).

"Be kind and compassionate to one another, forgiving each other, just as in Christ God forgave you" (Ephesians 4:32 NIV).

I can do all things [which He has called me to do] through Him who strengthens and empowers me [to fulfill His purpose—I am self-sufficient in Christ's sufficiency; I am ready for anything and equal to anything through Him who infuses me with inner strength and confident peace.]

Philippians 4:13 (AMP)

But He has said to me, "My grace is sufficient for you [My lovingkindness and My mercy are more than enough—always available—regardless of the situation]; for [My] power is being perfected [and is completed and shows itself most effectively] in [your] weakness." Therefore, I will all the more gladly boast in my weaknesses, so that the power of Christ [may completely enfold me and] may dwell in me.

2 Corinthians 12:9 (AMP)

MINISTRY OF THE BRIDE

About seventeen years ago, I was fifty-one years old and sitting in church, and the pastor said, "You know what God saved you from, but have you ever asked Him what He saved you for?" I was thinking about that as I walked into my living room after church, and I said, "God, I want to know what you saved me for. Is there anything that I can do for you?" As I was walking through, He gave me a vision of me standing in a large church speaking to hundreds of people, and I was wearing a beautiful wedding gown and veil, and my hair was long. I said, "God, what does that mean?" No answer. For three weeks, I saw that picture in my head. One day as I was walking through that same spot in the house, I heard God say, "I will answer you. My church is my bride, and my bride is not walking before me in faithfulness. I want you to put on the gown and veil and go tell them what I said." I said, "Lord, I can't do that. I'm old, I'm uneducated, and I'm a woman, and here in the south, that is not very accepted." I went to church the next Sunday, and a man with the gift of prophecy in my church came up to me. I had said nothing. He said, "Do not let the fact of your age, education, or the fact that you are a woman stop you. Go do what God has told you to do." I tried. I worked on notes and scriptures with God for weeks. I found a dress. I borrowed my daughter's veil and sent out a lot of letters with my notes and scriptures, and asked pastors to let me come. One response. The pastor at the small church where I had been saved and baptized years before that I had known all of his life gave me a date. I went on a Sunday morning with a packed house. I was praying, "Father, hide me behind the cross so Satan can't use me. Speak through me whatever You want to say to these people. I will be Your voice." I was so nervous until I got about two feet away from the pulpit, and then nothing had ever felt more right. As I went through my notes, all of a sudden, I was telling my testimony of when I had tried to kill myself. It was never a thought in my mind to tell that story. I had no intention of telling it; it was just flowing out of me. As I looked into the audience, He showed me who it was for. After I finished my message, I turned the service back over to the pastor for the altar call. He put anointing oil on my hands, and people came forward. One man came to the altar with his wife, and I prayed for her and their struggling marriage, and the lady that God had shown me came forward and asked me to pray for her. She did not mention suicide, and neither did I, but we prayed, and she seemed fine when she left. I went back to that church a year later and did a women's ministry day. The lady was still attending church there, and she came up to me and said, "You will never know what you did for me last year." I said, "I do know what God did for you. He showed me, and I'm so glad that you are still here." God is good. I didn't get many speaking engagements. Pastors are not very open to sharing their pulpits, especially with a woman, but God knew. He uses us where and when people allow. He is always at work in our lives. Before the ministry of the Bride, I was teaching sex education God's way to youth groups. One Wednesday night, I had spoken at a church and didn't have time to change clothes before going in to work at my third shift job. As I went to trade places with her at shift change, a lady at work said, "Where have you been?" (because I had on nice clothing). I told her, and she asked what I spoke on. I told her and explained the way that I taught it. She said, "I am a fifty-year-old Christian who has not walked before God in faithfulness with my sex life. Go tell those kids that this message just changed my life."

> "Therefore, since we are surrounded by such a great cloud of witnesses, let us throw off everything that hinders and the sin that so easily entangles. And let us run with perseverance the race marked out for us" (Hebrews 12:1 NIV).

> "He came as a witness to testify concerning that light, so that through him all might believe" (John 1:7 NIV).

> "I thank Christ Jesus our Lord, who has given me strength, that he considered me trustworthy, appointing me to his service" (1 Timothy 1:12 NIV).

FEAR IS A LIAR AND CAN CRIPPLE US

As I taught on the ministry of the Bride, God showed me a web page with me on it in a wedding gown and veil and the name of the ministry, but I let fear keep me from it. I had been told for many years that I was stupid and couldn't do anything right, and I was struggling to overcome it. During that time, I was working third shift in one of the carpet mills. One day, while I was at work at 5:30 a.m. on a Tuesday, God began to speak. We were going to Pigeon Forge, Tennessee, for a family reunion that Saturday for my dad's side of the family, and God said to me, "When you go to the reunion, I want you to be a witness for me." I said, okay. He said, "In the wedding dress." I said, "Lord, it's going to be hot, and we will be outside in the pavilion. That dress is heavy." The train felt like it weighed fifty pounds. He said, "But will you do it for me?" I didn't want to. I said, "Lord, the dress hasn't been cleaned. It has a big spot of olive oil on the front, and there's no time to get it cleaned." He said, "I don't want you to get it cleaned." I said, "You want me to wear a dirty dress?" He said, "Yes. I want them to see the spot, and I want you to tell them, 'My church is spotted, and I'm coming back for a church without spot or wrinkle.'" I said, "Okay, Lord." I did it. Most of my family treated me like I had leprosy after

I spoke, but I had a distant cousin there that I did not know. He talked to me afterward, and he got the message. It was for him. He was a new pastor. I always prayed and told God that if it just helped one person, I would do it; it would be worth it.

> "For the Spirit God gave us does not make us timid, but gives us power, love and self-discipline" (2 Timothy 1:7 NIV).

Ephesians 5 (read the whole chapter)

IF GOD TELLS YOU TO DO SOMETHING, HE HAS YOUR BACK

After we returned from Germany the second time and after my husband and I divorced, I worked in a small factory. I had known the owner for years. I had worked for him before marrying and being moved around everywhere with the army. The owner had told me if I ever came back, to come back to work for him, so I did, for several years.

While working there, I injured my neck, shoulder, and collarbone, trying to push a large roll of carpet off the roll-up. It was caught on one end. I put my shoulder under it and pushed up. I suffered for over a year. I went for therapy, which eased the pain, but didn't remove it and my other job duties aggravated it. I was on one side of the tufting machine, and the operator was on the other. I would have to yell for my operator several times a night to come and help me get the roll off. The boss's brother was an agitator, and he would mock me calling the operator's name and make fun of me. I think he didn't believe that I was really hurt. This went on for over a year. I begged him to stop. He was driving everyone crazy, mocking me every night that we worked—which was five to six nights a week. I was a single mom with a dead-beat husband who only paid a little child support when he thought he was going to get arrested, so I was under a lot of stress and in pain. People I worked with told me if I would get the boss's brother for harassment, they would go to court and testify. Not only were they sick of hearing it, but they also hated to see him abuse me. His brother would get on to him, but he had no respect for anyone and wouldn't quit. I asked him and pleaded with him to stop.

The owner came in and heard it one night and told the boss, "You better stop your brother from harassing her that way." It did no good. One night it was so bad. I was tired and in pain, and I wanted him to stop, and I asked him to, and he said, "I'm not doing anything, and nobody can stop me." As I walked away, I was on my way to the women's restroom, and I said to God, "Do I have to keep putting up with this, or is there anything I can do?" As I was washing my hands in the women's room, the Lord said to me, "He needs his mouth washed out with soap. Do it." We used lava soap, which is gritty and rough (to remove the machine grease). The soap bar was melted and soft on the bottom. I took a handful of paper towels and wet them and folded them, and rubbed a thick paste of soap from the bottom of the bar. I was fearing and trembling when I headed that way. I thought this guy was going to knock me forty feet. I was shaking. When I got to his machine, he was standing like a concrete statue with his mouth open when I put the soap in his mouth. He didn't even twitch or bat an eyelash until I was about six feet away from him. He started spitting and took off to his brother—the boss. I went back to my machine, thinking I would be fired any minute. In a few minutes, here comes the boss. He asked, "What did you do to him? He said you threw something in his face." He couldn't imagine me getting that close to him and him not stopping me. He didn't realize what had happened. Our God delivers us (Psalms 34:19). I told his brother (the boss), "You were told to handle this, and you didn't, so it's handled. Now he will leave me alone." I was afraid he would ask the owner for permission to fire me. The next day I went to see if I was going to be fired. I didn't want to be fired in front of all the people that I worked with, so I went to see the owner. I asked him if I was going to be fired, and he said, "Why on earth would you think that?" I told him what I did. He busted out laughing, got up, came around the desk, and said, "I want to shake your hand. Don't worry. You won't have any more trouble out of him, and your job is secure." Again, I say Psalm 34:19, and I had no more trouble from him.

> "The righteous person may have many troubles, but the Lord delivers him from them all" (Psalm 34:19 NIV).

As a disclaimer: Anyone facing workplace harassment should report it to their superior immediately and go through the proper channels to handle the situation. I do not condone revenge.

A Sermon We All Need

A very wise pastor that we had many years ago preached a very helpful sermon one time that it took me twenty-five years, I'm sad to say, to get it. He said many medicines have to be shaken well to get the good out of them, and so do people. When God shakes you, what comes out? A sweet fragrance, a good medicine, a healing balm? Some plants and trees have to be crushed and broken to get good medicine or sweet fragrance out of them. What comes out of us when we are crushed and broken? My son, who was ten years old at the time, said, "That's the best message preacher Darey has ever preached." I didn't think he was listening. He was doodling on a paper, but he was quiet and not bothering his sister. On the way home from church, he recalled the whole message. I would cringe at it over the years as I would mess up, get a bad attitude, and offend someone and say, "God, am I ever going to get this right?" I finally realized that it is a daily thing. We have to ask God daily to guard our mouths, thoughts, and actions. Trust me when I say that when I don't pray it, I'll usually pay for it. It's best to turn ourselves over to Him daily as soon as we wake up. If we do, our day goes by so much better.

"Listen to my voice in the morning, Lord. Each morning I bring my requests to you and wait expectantly" (Psalm 5:3 NLT).

"O God, you are my God; I earnestly search for you. My soul thirsts for you; my whole body longs for you in this parched and weary land where there is no water" (Psalm 63:1 NLT).

"Finally, brothers and sisters, whatever is true, whatever is noble, whatever is right, whatever is pure, whatever is lovely, whatever is admirable—if anything is excellent or praiseworthy—think about such things" (Philippians 4:8 NIV).

"But you are a chosen people, a royal priesthood, a holy nation, God's special possession, that you may declare the praises of him who called you out of darkness into his wonderful light" (1 Peter 2:9 NIV).

BUS MINISTRY

In the late 1980s, I was encouraging a friend named Janie. We would do church visitation together. She was thinking about driving a church van, and I encouraged her mightily, not feeling at all that I could do it, but I was sure that she could. We both did it in our years together at that church. We had some great moments—visitation, bus ministry, AWANA, and VBS. I miss those days, but I have beautiful memories. One day on visitation, we were at a grandmother's house and met her granddaughter, who was nine years old, and her little brother, who was about three. He could barely climb on the church van but wanted no help. They told us where they lived and said they wanted to come to church, so I began to pick them up. They loved church. As they got a little older, the little boy came less and less, but the young girl was faithful. She would tell me that she loved me and that I helped her. She would say, "Vickie, you have no idea how long it is from Sunday to Wednesday and from Wednesday to Sunday." I was a single mom, working three jobs to keep a roof over our heads. I thank God for my sister Rosie who helped us in that endeavor. I always wished I could do more but couldn't seem to manage. Their mom was a night manager at a minute market, and their dad worked in one of the carpet mills. One Wednesday night at church, we were in the Sunday School building behind the church with no phone.

The weather was getting rough, and one of the deacons came and called me to the phone. None of us had cell phones back then. It was the little boy and girl's dad. He said, "Vickie, they won't let my wife or me off work, and there is a tornado warning tonight. Will you please take my kids home with you tonight?" I did. I took them to get clothes and bedded them down on my couch. God kept us all safe. I prayed with them for our safety and their parents' safety. I assured them that I felt God would take care of us all, and He did. The boy stopped coming when he was about eleven or twelve years old, or he rarely came, but every time I brought his sister home, he would come out to the van and talk to me. I would have to just finally say, "I've got to go." It was his thirteenth birthday, and I pulled into their yard. I think it was a Sunday evening. It was still a little light out. He came to the van as usual, but he said, "Vickie, today's my birthday." I wished him a happy birthday, and I said, "I just got a new CD. This is the first time I've ever played it. I'm going to give this to you." It was a Third Day CD. He let me know later that he loved it. He started attending another church and growing in Jesus. I rarely saw him, and then one day I was in the dollar store, and someone came and did a Spider-Man leap in front of me. It was him. We were both very excited to see each other. He was fifteen or sixteen at that time. I said, "Are you still in church?" He said, "Yes, and it's because of you." He said, "Remember the CD that you gave me? It changed my life." I later found out that he was at school and started talking to a boy about the CD and how he had come to love contemporary music. The boy was the one who invited him to church.

Later the boy moved away, but he kept going. He was seventeen. One day I got a call from his sister, and she said that their mom had just died of an asthma attack, and her brother wanted me to come. His mom died in his arms as they waited for an ambulance. They could not get her back. I would see them on occasion. I had moved when the girl was eighteen, and she, at some point, had gotten out of church. Life was very hard for her. She birthed two children and had a failed marriage. The last time I saw her, she still wasn't doing well. Her brother did well in school and went on to college. I used to run into him in Walmart late at night. We would talk for at least two hours each time. We exchanged phone numbers and one day he came over with his girlfriend, and we had a meal together, and then another, and then he was telling me his big plan to propose and asked me if I would make their wedding cake and groom's cake. I did. Both of them were still in college, and life has gotten busy for all of us. I've not seen them lately, but I need to reconnect and see how they're doing. His dad told me at the wedding that he was still in church, but I could see he was still struggling. I pray they are all doing well.

> "Jesus said, 'Let the children come to me, and do not hinder them, for the kingdom of heaven belongs to such as these'" (Matthew 19:14 NIV).

MY MISSION FIELD

I was sitting in church one Sunday night, and God gave me a vision during prayer time. He showed me my co-workers and told me that the people I worked with were my mission field. That was over thirty years ago, and it is still the same. Some of the people that I met on that job all those years ago are still in my life and call me for prayer. People keep asking me, "When are you going to retire?" I am in my late sixties and can't imagine retiring because God still uses me in the workplace. It is still my mission field. Wherever we do life, that is our mission field. We are not all called to foreign soil. Ask God to live, breathe, and love through you every day and to use you wherever you are, and He will, in the most unexpected places and unexpected conversations.

> "Wherefore thou art great, O Lord God: for there is none like thee, neither is there any God beside thee, according to all that we have heard with our ears" (2 Samuel 7:22 KJV).

MY FIRST YOUTH CAMP

When my children were ten and twelve, the twelve-year-old was just starting into the youth group. I had helped in Sunday School, children's church, and AWANA, but I had not been involved with the youth yet. They needed people to go to youth camp as workers, and I told them I was afraid of teenagers, that I didn't know how to relate to them. They kept begging me to go, and I said, "Okay, I will work in the kitchen." We were going to leave on a Monday morning, and on the Saturday morning before, God gave me a vision. Two sisters were going, thirteen and fifteen, Rebecca and Rachel. I had a vision of me standing with one of them on either side of me, and I pulled them to me in a hug, and I heard God say loud and clear, "When it happens, handle it with love," and the vision disappeared. I thought, "What was that?" I didn't understand. We left on Monday morning, sixty-one of us, and went to Gatlinburg, TN, for youth camp. We were all in one building. On the second day, I was in the kitchen helping make dinner. The kids had been down to Gatlinburg with all the youth leaders. Some of the kids were walking ahead of them and got back first, and were in the building. Someone yelled that there was fighting upstairs. Another woman went up with me. I pulled one girl one way, and she pulled the other girl the other way. It was the two sisters—Rebecca and Rachel. The rules were that if there was a fight, they had to take the kids home right then—someone would drive them back home. I had the fifteen-year-old. She was angry and crying and said, "I hate my sister. I have hated her since the day she was born. I will always hate her. I want to go home now." She was embarrassed. God said, "Do not let them send these girls home." I said to her, "You are not going home. You are going to stay here with people who love you, and we're going to help you work this out." She said, "If you don't send me home, I will do something bad where you will have to." I said, "If you do, I will spank you like you were mine, and you will still stay." (I knew I could've gotten in a lot of trouble for that, but God told me not to let them leave.) I heard the pastor and youth pastor coming up the stairs. I went and met them and said, "God told me not to let these girls go home. I know we are supposed to, but God said, 'Don't.'" They took the two girls in a room with me and the other lady who broke them up. The youth pastor, his wife, the other lady, and I had one on each bunk, and we were sitting with the two girls. The youth pastor had them talk about what happened and what was going on. He told them that he wanted them to stay if they would agree to leave each other alone and leave each other's stuff alone for the rest of the week. After he finished talking to them, he looked at the other lady and me and said, "Do either of you have anything you want to say?" I said, "Girls, do you think that God makes mistakes?" They both said no. I said, "Then he didn't make a mistake when he put you in the same family and made you sisters." They dropped their heads. They knew I had them. I said, "One day, you are going to love and appreciate each other and be thankful to have one another." We all got up to go downstairs to have dinner. As we stood up, I did what God showed me in the vision—I pulled both girls to me in a hug. They didn't resist. I told them that I loved them, and we all went downstairs.

After dinner, we all gathered in a huge circle in the main room. As the band started the worship music, a ten-year-old boy had come with his mother and sister, got up and started going around the room, hugging everybody. When he did, the Spirit of God came down in that place. The older sister, who said that she hated her sister, got up, walked across the room, hugged her sister, and told her that she loved her. The Spirit broke out, and no one ever preached, but eight kids got saved. The thirteen-year-old was one of them. The youth pastor's wife looked back at the books from the year before, and the fifteen-year-old had gotten saved on that same day the year before. That's what the devil was trying to stop. That is one night the devil didn't win. Thank you, Jesus, for that experience. I was a youth leader for years after that. Working with the youth is one thing that I miss more than anything other than raising my kids. To God, be the Glory!

> "For it is with your heart that you believe and are justified, and it is with your mouth that you profess your faith and are saved" (Romans 10:10 NIV).

> "Restore to me the joy of Your salvation, and uphold me by Your generous Spirit" (Psalm 51:12 NKJV).

TODAY IS THE DAY OF SALVATION

As I was working in the Christian bookstore one afternoon, a young man came in. I was standing over by the *Left Behind* book display. It was in the late 1990s. They were best-sellers at the time. He approached me and asked about the Bible on CD, and he began to tell me that two weeks earlier, he had gone to church with his cousin, and during the altar call, his cousin went forward and gave his life to Jesus. He said he had felt Jesus tugging at his heart, and he wished he had gone forward with his cousin and asked Him into his heart. I said to him, "The Bible says that today is the day of salvation. You can ask Him into your heart right now if you want. I'll be honored to pray with you." He said yes. I led him to Jesus right there. He was a truck driver. I never saw him again, but I know I will someday. I will be in his welcoming reunion when he crosses over to heaven. Oh, happy day.

> "For He says, 'At the acceptable time (the time of grace) I listened to you, And I helped you on the day of salvation.' Behold, now is 'the acceptable time,' behold, now is 'the day of salvation'" (2 Corinthians 6:2 NASB).

But in your hearts set Christ apart [as holy—acknowledging Him, giving Him first place in your lives] as Lord. Always be ready to give a [logical] defense to anyone who asks you to account for the hope and confident assurance [elicited by faith] that is within you, yet [do it] with gentleness and respect.

1 Peter 3:15 (AMP)

BEARING FRUIT

One Saturday night in 2000 or 2001, I went to a Steven Curtis Chapman concert, and they talked about the movie "Through the Gates of Splendor." They showed some of the footage from the movie and had one of the tribe members there. As I left there that night, I went home crying, saying, "God, I haven't done anything for You lately. I've been in a dry season, and I'm tired of the dry season." I never spoke the words out of my mouth, just in my heart to God. I was attending a new church. I had only been going there for about three weeks. The next day after the concert was Sunday. I went to church, and at the altar call, I went forward. I knelt on my knees, and I said again to God, "I am tired of this dry season. I want to do something for You again. God, I would love to hear a message from You." There were ladies kneeling and praying on both sides of me—praying for me, I think. They didn't touch me or speak. Then I felt them leave, and I felt a big hand take my hand. I looked up at a very large Middle Eastern man, and he said, "I have a message for you from the Most High God, 'Don't worry about the dry season. You will bear fruit again, and it will be much fruit.'" I thanked him, and he said, "Don't thank me. I am just obeying God. This is the work that He gave me to do." I said, "I am thanking you for your obedience to Him." A week or two later, my daughter came into the church alone and sat down beside me weeping, and I said in my heart, "God, give this man a message for her, and send him to help her." He got up out of his seat during song service and gave her a message that spoke directly to her need. Her husband was going through a time when he didn't want to go to church. The message the man gave her was, "Continue to do what you know is right, and God will deal with your husband." A year or so later, one of my nieces and her brother lived on the same property in separate houses. They were having a lot of problems. She said one Sunday that a big Middle Eastern man came to their church and came to her and said, "You and your brother are having a lot of trouble, but God is working on it, and it's going to be okay." I know who that man was, and I thanked God that he had a messenger willing to go. My niece said they had not spoken to anyone at their church about that problem, and this man was a visitor (or was he an angel?).

> "And so it was with me, brothers and sisters. When I came to you, I did not come with eloquence or human wisdom as I proclaimed to you the testimony about God" (1 Corinthians 2:1 NIV).

> "Search me, God, and know my heart; test me and know my anxious thoughts" (Psalm 139:23 NIV).

BE READY

I was invited to speak at another church one Saturday morning to a ladies' group. I had confirmed three days before with the lady who invited me. On my way to the church, I said, "Lord, if there are three or thirty, reach down to the one who is hurting the most and meet their need." As I was driving, the devil spoke to me and said, "You know you can't do this." I answered him and said, "I know, but I know who can and will do it through me." As I pulled into the church twenty minutes before, there were only three vehicles in the parking lot, and one was a church van. I went to the door, and it was locked. I went to the fellowship hall, and it was locked. There was a bench in front of the church. I sat down on the bench and said, "Lord, you sent me here, so I'm going to wait." I started looking over my notes again, and a man opened the door from the inside and said, "Can I help you?" I told him that I was supposed to lead a Bible study there, and I told him the lady's name that had invited me. He told me that there was no one there but him and a church sister and that they were getting ready for homecoming tomorrow. He told me that I could go into the kitchen and talk to her while he called the lady who invited me. I went into the kitchen and began to talk to this lady who I had never met. She was so broken. Her husband had left her and her children for another woman. He wasn't helping to support them. They

173

were struggling so hard. She began to weep as she told me the story. The other lady came in who had invited me and said, "Let's go in this room, and we can talk." As the lady wept, God just poured words of ministry through me to her. When He was through, she said to me, "I was so far down I didn't even think God loved me anymore, but He sent you." The other lady said, "I needed that message as much as she did. Our whole church needs that message." She never explained what happened and why they didn't have the Bible study, but God sent me there, and she never contacted me to come back. She had been working with me and changed jobs before I went to go speak there, but God had a plan and a purpose that day, and it was the broken lady. I thank Him for flowing through me to meet her need.

> "For My thoughts are not your thoughts, Nor are your ways My ways," says the Lord. For as the heavens are higher than the earth, so are My ways higher than your ways, and My thoughts than your thoughts" (Isaiah 55:8-9 NKJV).

JESUS THE HITCHHIKER

This is not my story, but it needs to be told. My pastor told me this story about a deacon that he knew. A man was training another man on the bread route to drive a bread truck. One of them was a deacon in the church. They were on Shallowford Road in Chattanooga, Tennessee. As they were driving the bread route, they saw a hitchhiker. They knew they were not allowed to put anyone else in the bread truck, but they both had the overwhelming feeling that they must pick this guy up. By the time they decided to stop, they had already passed him. They turned around and went back. They picked him up, and he was sitting behind them in the bread truck. They were talking about their church, their families, and their lives as one was training the other on the route. The man leaned up between them and said, "It's good to know you are about the Father's business." He then disappeared before their eyes. The driver pulled off the road, and they were looking at each other in shock, thinking about what had just happened when a state trooper pulled over to see if they were okay or if they were broke down. They told him what happened, and he began to weep. They asked him what was wrong, and he said, "You are the fifth person who has told me that story today."

Jesus will give anyone a minute. Ask for it.

"Be not forgetful to entertain strangers: for thereby some have entertained angels unawares" (Hebrews 13:2 KJV).

And some even entertain a Savior—a risen King.

Looking for a White Jeep

When I became a grandmother, I started thinking about a larger vehicle. I was considering a van, but my son said that I should buy a Jeep. I said okay, and he told me that it needed a certain engine and that it was the best engine that Jeep ever made, so I decided that I wanted a white Jeep Grand Cherokee. I went and looked at a few used ones, but I couldn't find what I wanted. We had searched on a couple of Saturdays and had not found anything. Just as I was waking up on a Saturday morning, I heard God tell me where to go to look for my Jeep. I was lying there in the bed, amazed that He had told me where to go find my Jeep, and my son called and said, "Mom, I'm off today. Do you want to go look for your Jeep?" I said, "Come on over. I know where we are going." There it was. The only white one on the lot, with the right engine and everything that I had wanted. They gave me a good deal, and I drove home happy. As I laid down to go to sleep that night, I said, "Oh my God, I'm on four days at work, and I just bought the most expensive vehicle that I've ever bought. What was I thinking?" Immediately I heard God say, "I helped you pay for the last one, didn't I?" and He had. He had always provided extra work at times when I needed it. He is a good Father. He wants to hear from us, to hear our voice. Talk to Him. Tell Him what you need and want and believe.

> "It is good to give thanks to the Lord, and to sing praises to Your name, O Most High. To declare Your lovingkindness in the morning, and Your faithfulness every night" (Psalm 92:1-2 NKJV).

As a disclaimer: If you need a different vehicle for some reason—growing family, need a truck to haul stuff, etc.—pray for favor. I am not saying to go out and buy an expensive vehicle because you want it and ask God to help you make the payments. Use wisdom.

RESCUE IN THE SNOW

It was the winter of 2004. I lived forty-five minutes away from my job. I would go over a small mountain instead of going the long way around to get to the interstate. I worked second shift. I left work early one night because it was snowing pretty heavily. As I started to go home, I felt an overbearing pressure from God to go across the mountain, but I knew that I couldn't drive down the other side of the mountain safely. It would have been suicide. I would have slid off the mountain. My Jeep was already sliding on the road, just driving 30 mph. I was used to a small car with front-wheel drive. I had never driven the Jeep in the snow before. I kept saying to God, "Why are you making me go to the mountain? You know I am not going to go down the other side." I started to turn around several times. There was no one on the road. The snow was getting heavier, but I felt a force greater than my own pushing me on, and I said to God several more times, "God, why are we going up this mountain? You know I'm not driving down the other side. I don't understand this." As I started the grade up the mountain, there was a car stopped. I pulled up beside it and rolled down my window. It was the husband of one of my nieces. He said, "Vickie, my tires are worn slick, and I'm afraid to go over that mountain, but I don't have enough gas to turn back and get to the gas station." I said, "I know a shortcut to another place where you can get gas." I told him to go up a little further, and there would be a spot to turn around and that I would turn around, and he could follow me. We went to the gas station together and then took the interstate home. We both made it home safe. I am so glad that I obeyed God and kept going. I have never felt such a forcefulness from God. I did not feel that I had a choice, and I could not see the reasoning, but praise God, I obeyed.

> "Even there your hand will guide me, your right hand will hold me fast" (Psalm 139:10 NIV).

> "Lead me by your truth and teach me, for you are the God who saves me. All day long I put my hope in you" (Psalm 25:5 NLT).

A Sweet Fragrance, an Open Door

Being a mom was, aside from my salvation, the greatest joy in my life. I loved every stage. My kids were a wonderful blessing and gave me purpose and enrichment. Then came the empty nest. By the time they were sixteen, I would cry at the thought of the day they would leave home. How could I manage without seeing their faces or hearing their voices? My son married and left home first, then my daughter. It was painful. I had started attending a new church and found some new friends. I began to hear in my spirit, "for such a time as this" (Esther 4:14). Our group of friends was talking one night after church about some concerns we had for a particular area we worked with at the church. I decided to fast and pray that night at work. I worked third shift from 11 p.m. to 7 a.m. The Lord said, "You are here for such a time as this." I felt we needed to get together and pray. I called them, they called their friends, and they said that we could meet at their house. I told them that l would bring food. We got together and prayed, and then the Friday night fellowship began. The ministry in that place each week was great. Our heavenly Father did so very much in all of our lives. To everything, there is a time and a season. We helped make some changes that needed to be made in the church (for such a time as this), and some of us moved on to other churches. It was God's timing again. To everything, there is a time and season. Most of us can look back and see many times and seasons in our lives. This one left many wonderful memories and a few sad ones—some of us had loved ones pass away. Once a month at the Friday night fellowship, we started having a birthday party for the attendees who had a birthday that month. We had thirty-five to fifty people for most weeks. We had themed parties—some of them, I'm ashamed to say, got a little bit worldly. I'm not pleased with myself as I look back on my conduct on some of those occasions—I'm ashamed. We have to be on guard. The enemy is always at work, looking for an opportunity when we are off guard. But I did see Jesus move in that place, and a lot of people grow in Him. There were a lot of life-changing moments when God showed up, and miracles happened. It was always a great place to be. We had lots of good people and a great band. We sang and ate and had devotion and prayer. It was a beautiful season in our lives for several years there.

One Friday night, we had a lot of visitors, and the place was full. At the end of the devotion, we all joined hands to pray. As we finished, the Lord told me to give a testimony of a time that I had tried to take my life. I didn't want to, and He told me again to do it, so I said, "The Lord told me to share this testimony," and I did. I said, "Whoever is here thinking these thoughts of suicide, it is the enemy trying to rob you of all that God has planned for you. If I had died, I would be in hell now. I would have missed Jesus, heaven, and all God had planned for me, my children, and my grandchildren." I had just become a grandmother. I said, "I am so thankful I did not die. Don't listen to that negative voice. Don't do it. Live. God has a plan just for you." We broke up the circle and ate some more and fellowshipped to the band music (that we were so blessed to have). One person sacrificed a lot for us to have a band. Two people gave up their home each week for us all to meet and enjoy. And our band members came and gave their time and talent for our enjoyment. It was such a beautiful, warm, welcoming place to be. This couple had birds, dogs, cats, horses, a fish pond, and two very big hearts with a lot of love to give. Thank you both. I love you two to the heavens always and forever. I'm so thankful for the seasons we shared, and so many others would echo that love and gratefulness.

As the evening went on, I walked over to a table of four new guests and welcomed them. One of the ladies said, "You said God spoke to you." I said, "Yes, I did." She said, "I've been a Christian for years, and I've never heard God speak." I said to her, "I'm sure you have. We often think it's our own thoughts, but as fathers talk to their children, so does God. We don't see Him, so we are not listening, but if we believe He speaks and we listen, we will hear Him. We're so busy we're not looking for Him to show up or speak. He is talking. We are missing it. Listen, ask Him to speak to you, tell Him you want to hear His voice, and you will."

As the night was ending, most everyone was gone; I was gathering my dishes to go. Someone said to me, "I'll help you." I said, "I'm a mom. I'm used to having my hands full." He replied, "I will help you." I said okay, and when we got to the car, I told him to put the dishes he had on the floor of the car, and I was putting some behind the driver's seat. I raised up just as his head landed on my shoulders. He simply said, "It's me." I was shocked. We can be drowning in pain and paste a smile on our face and go on, but at some point, we run into the wall. This person was serious. He was about to take his life. He had put everything in his wife's name and had his letter written. The enemy had convinced him that he was a failure. What a lie! He had so much life and ministry going on. Whatever the enemy is telling you is a lie. He never speaks the truth. The Bible calls him the father of lies. I prayed and talked to him for a few minutes and made him promise to talk to his wife and not to harm himself. His wife called me that week and asked me if I would talk with him. I said I would meet them at their house when they were both at home. We didn't get to that week. He seemed to be doing okay on Friday night when I saw him at the fellowship. On Sunday, I went out of town to visit a cousin who was in prison. I was heading home, and I thought, "If I hurry, I can run into the church and catch the message." It was already after 6 p.m. I had been up since 6 a.m. and was supposed to go to work at 11 p.m. The Lord spoke to me and said, "No, go talk to this man. He needs you to talk to him now." I said, "Lord, fill me with your words." I was there by 6:45 p.m. His wife showed us to the living room. She said I'll be in the bedroom reading if you need me. I ended up calling work, saying that I couldn't come in at 11 p.m. His wife had joined us, and we prayed until 1:30 a.m. We parted after the three of us had a serious prayer time on the living room floor. I think it was Tuesday night in that same living room that he led his son and daughter-in-law to Jesus and saved a marriage that is still together so many years later. The enemy could have messed that family up badly.

We all go through times in our lives that are tough. No one was ever meant to live life alone. We need family, friends, and acquaintances to make us whole, and we definitely need Jesus in our hearts and the Holy Spirit working in our lives.

We need people to put an arm around our shoulder and say, "Are you doing okay today?" Don't ever let the enemy get you away to yourself when you are down. Call someone, take a walk in the sunshine, look up. Life is worth living, and when you get through your rough spot, you can help others through theirs. We all go through many dark days and nights. We are blessed this day and age to have cell phones so we can reach out to someone and say, "I need to talk. Can you lend an ear and a prayer?" We have a friend in the Lord Jesus Christ, and if all ears are busy, He is willing to listen anytime day or night. He said, "I have come that you may have life" (John 10:10). "My peace I give unto you" (John 14:27).

> "I have told you these things, so that in me you may have peace. In this world, you will have trouble. But take heart! I have overcome the world" (John 16:33 NIV).

> "And the peace of God, which transcends all understanding, will guard your hearts and your minds in Christ Jesus" (Philippians 4:7 NIV).

> "Whoever pursues righteousness and love finds life, prosperity and honor" (Proverbs 21:21 NIV).

> "I have told you this so that my joy may be in you and that your joy may be complete" (John 15:11 NIV).

We have so many promises in the Word of God. The Word gives us strength, and it is our defense against the enemy. Jesus, when he was tempted by Satan after fasting for forty days, said, "It is written…" (Matthew 4). He used the Word against Satan, so we would know to do the same. He is our example. The Word is our instruction book. Yes, we struggle. We have an enemy of our souls. He cannot take our salvation, but he is a devious foe—desperate to stop us from reaching our destinies in Christ and to make us ineffective. He is always messing with us and trying to make us think something is wrong with us or we are not enough. He distracts us to keep us from being an effective witness for Jesus Christ. When the enemy comes around, nothing feels right. The atmosphere around us changes. Rebuke him, throw him out, and say every demon in hell get out of my house and away from me in the name of Jesus. Sing, listen to Christian music. If you play it in your house 24/7, the demons won't come around. They cannot inhabit the praises of God. Sing Him a love song. I like to sing these lyrics by Van Morrison like I am singing to Jesus: *Have I told You lately that I love You / Have I told You (Lord) there's no one else above You / You fill my heart with gladness. / You take away all of my sadness. / You ease my troubles, yes You do.* Lord, I can't make it without You. Pour your heart out to the One who went to the whipping post for your healing and to the cross for your salvation and deliverance. Wow, what a friend we have in Jesus. Love on Him, sing to Him, live for Him. Oh, what a Savior, our Redeemer, our strength when we have none. Call on Him. He is there. Crawl up in His lap. You are His child if you give your heart to Him. Do it now. Just say, "Jesus, I am a sinner. I sinned against You. I ask for Your forgiveness. Come into my heart and be my savior." He will. Learn His word. Read the book of John. Read Psalm 23 and Psalm 91.

"For God so loved the world that he gave his one and only Son, that whoever believes in him shall not perish but have eternal life. For God did not send his Son into the world to condemn the world, but to save the world through him" (John 3:16-17 NIV).

Sing, "Jesus loves me, this I know, for the Bible tells me so. Oh, how He loves you and me, oh how He loves you and me. He gave His life. What more could He give. Oh, how He loves you, oh, how He loves me. Oh, how He loves you and me." He wants to spend eternity with you, and so do I. Shut your ears to the enemy with all his negativity. Listen to your Savior. He will talk to you. Now you have a story to tell. Go tell it. Say, "In the name of Jesus, I'm going to live and tell it. Amen."

SET UP BY GOD

About sixteen or seventeen years ago, our work was down to four days, and I needed to pick up some extra work. This girl from church told me about a couple of people who were homebound and needed help, so I started first with a lady who had been in bed for twenty years. She had a service that came in and always checked on her, but they didn't do cleaning, clearing, or run errands. I worked probably six to eight hours a week for her, at $5 an hour. Then, the girl from church sent me to a couple who wanted someone to come cook a couple of dinners a week, clean up the kitchen, and wash a load of laundry while I cooked. The first day I prepared the meal and served them at the kitchen table, and the lady asked me to say a blessing over the food. I did. It seemed to bother her husband, and he said nothing. One day as I cooked, he came into the kitchen and sat down. It was a small kitchen. We could easily talk because his wife was out on the patio smoking. He told me that the doctor told him he only had a short time to live. He had prostate cancer. I sat down and told him that I was sorry and that it would be painful to hear such a report. I asked if I could pray, and he said no. He said, "I have a friend who's a preacher, and he knows I don't want to talk about this stuff." I said, "Okay. Is there anything else I can do? I will write letters and cards or make phone calls if you would like. If there's something you

want to do or somewhere you want to go, I will try to help."
He said, "No. There's nothing." About a week later, I was
making dinner, and his daughter had taken him to the doctor. They did some sort of prostate procedure. He was in pain
and miserable. He went to the restroom. He said there was
too much blood. His daughter wanted to take him back to
the hospital, but he refused and told her to go on home to
her family and that he would be okay. She reluctantly left. He
went into the living room and laid down on the sofa. I had
their dinner on the table. His wife was ready to eat. He said
he couldn't eat right then, and I offered to bring it to him, to
get him soup, anything. He said no. His wife and I ate, and I
covered his plate and put it away. I went to check on him. He
was chilling and in pain. I got him a blanket and asked him
if I could pray for him. This time he said yes. I knelt down
and laid hands on him and prayed and went back to clean the
kitchen. In a few minutes, he was up and looking through
stuff and getting around fine. I said, "Can I help you find
something?" He knew I love to bake. He said, "I'm looking
for something to give you." I said, "You don't need to give me
anything." He pulled out a new three-pound can of butter
flavor Crisco. He said, "This will help you with your baking."
He insisted that I take it, so I did. He declined pretty rapidly
after that. Soon he was in a wheelchair, and hospice was coming and checking on him, I think, three times a week. His
legs began to fill with fluid. It was hard for him to go from
his wheelchair to his living room chair, but he wanted to, so
we did. Sometimes he would almost pull me down, and I
would say, "Hey, if we're going to two-step, you have to look
out for that third step," and he would chuckle. He was having to walk with the walker and be in the chair most of the
time. One day I helped him from the potty chair to the
wheelchair. He was already humiliated because he had to

have help. I told him most all of us are going to go through times like this in our lives and not to be embarrassed. I was who God provided to help. I didn't realize how much fluid he had in his legs. At that point, when he tried to move to the wheelchair, he failed. I was able to push him into the locked wheelchair before I went down. He was fine, praise God, and I only sustained some bruises. Again, praise God. They put him in the hospital, and I went to visit. I was there when the doctor called his daughter out to the hall with the door wide open. We could hear everything he told her. He said that her dad was not well and that it would only be days and he would not leave the hospital. He was upset, of course. No one wants to hear those words. I said, "May I pray with you?" and he said yes. We prayed, and I left telling him that I would be back. I came back in two days, and he had quit eating. He refused everything. I asked him if he wanted to go home, and he said yes. I told him if he would eat and get his strength, they would let him go home, and I would take off work and take care of him. I had no training. He knew, but he said yes, so we began a journey to the end. He lived for two more weeks. His daughters were amazing. We made it. Two nights before he died, he had a bad night. I slept on the floor beside his bed. I had been in the guest room across the hall for two weeks. He kept waking up during the night, asking me to put his legs back on the bed. He kept thinking they were falling off. I'm sure they felt like they were asleep. They were full of fluid. He did pretty well that last day. One of his grandsons came by during his dinner. He wasn't very hungry, but he was so shaky that I had to feed him. He was embarrassed and did not want to eat. I talked him into a little sherbet. He liked the rainbow sherbet. Then his grandson wheeled him out on the patio and stayed with him until he was ready for bed. When I took him back and helped him in the bed, he asked for medicines that hospice had left, but he had not been taking any. It was for pain and rest. He had said goodnight to his wife as we had started to his room. As I told him good night, he said good night to me and told me that he loved me. Those were his last words. I slept across the hall with both of our doors open. I think it was between two and three in the morning. I woke up thinking someone had come into the house because I could feel a presence. He was sleeping. I thought one of the children had come in. They had three girls. As I walked through the house, so did both dogs and the cat. They were looking too. We all felt someone, but no one was there. His wife was sound asleep, and he was too. That was the first time I had seen the animals go through the house like that. I should have known that it was the death angel, but I think the Lord knew his wife, and I needed to rest for a while before what was to come. I went back to bed at 6:30 a.m. I awoke to the sound of the death rattle. I had never heard it before but had heard of it, and I knew what it was. I went to his bed and said, "I know you can hear me, and just like you hear me, God can hear you. If there's anything you need to say to Him before you meet Him, now is the time, and He will hear you." There was total silence. I wasn't sure if he was still breathing, and then the death rattle started back and went on until I think it was about 8:30 a.m. Then he went to be with Jesus. At his viewing, we all learned a lot about his life story. He had worked for the railroad and near his work was a homeless camp. His family and I found out that he had given his lunch away almost every day to feed someone who was truly hungry. Viewings are so important. Many people don't do that anymore, but it helps give closure, and we learn so many things about our loved ones from friends, acquaintances, and co-workers. Everyone sees things differently. I thank God for the experience. If I had been asked to be his caregiver in the beginning, I would have said no. I would have been afraid. He said he had peace with God, but yet he was afraid to die. That's why I was there. I would tell him it would just be a step over. You give up a breath here and catch it on the other side, or you just take a step over. You won't be alone. It was an experience I thank God for but not one that I would have asked for. I did also help with his wife at her passing. Hospice offered me a job. I told them I couldn't handle the emotions of it all the time. It wasn't for me. They said if I ever changed my mind, I know how to find them. I've done many jobs, mostly at carpet mills. I still work in one. The Lord told me many years ago that my workplace is my mission field. Only He knows my next steps. I pray my footsteps will fit perfectly in His.

"For God hath not given us the spirit of fear; but of power, and of love, and of a sound mind" (2 Timothy 1:7 NKJV).

"In all thy ways acknowledge him, and he shall direct thy paths" (Proverbs 3:6 NKJV).

(The entire chapter is great. Read Proverbs chapter 3.)

BROTHER TERRY—HIS FIRST MIRACLE OF MANY

On February 4, 1960, my baby brother, Terry, was born. My mom said her midwife was a black lady, a strong woman of God. He was born in Fort Myers, but we still lived in Alva. He was born with the umbilical cord around his neck and was choked until his body was so blue that he looked black. She said she had never heard a woman pray like that midlife prayed as she worked with him to get him to breathe. Mama said it seemed like thirty minutes before he cried, but God answered those prayers, and my brother had no brain damage or problems. God is good. He did have asthma, like my mom, and that's why we ended up moving back to Georgia. The Florida heat was too hard on them. We were very poor, and I don't remember us even having a fan.

> "A psalm of David. Lord, hear my prayer, listen to my cry for mercy; in your faithfulness and righteousness come to my relief" (Psalm 143:1 NIV).

My Baby Brother Terry—An Accident Looking for a Place to Happen Always

My little brother, Terry, was delivered by a midwife in 1960. He was choked blue by the umbilical cord wrapped around his neck. My mom said it seemed like thirty minutes as the midwife worked with him to get him to breathe. She said she never heard a woman pray like that woman did. Finally, a cry and the joy of new life coming into the world. As a toddler, he had a pneumonia fever of 108. The doctor said he would have brain damage again. There was none. He had multiple childhood accidents. His arm got caught in an old washer. The wringer spun the skin off almost to the bone, and it healed up with no damage. He fell with an axe at five years old while taking it to our dad, and he cut his wrist badly. It healed fine the same year. He walked through an area, barefoot, when my dad had burned brush the day before and burned his feet badly on hot coals under the ashes. He healed fine. He was in a bad car wreck when he was nine or ten years old. He would have bled to death if a state trooper had not been involved in the accident and performed the right pressure in the right places. His nose and tongue were cut about half off. He had terrible cuts and abrasions to the face. His carotid artery down the right side of his neck was cut across in two places. I'm so thankful for the state trooper who was there to help him. There were two deaths and lots of serious injuries. Five cars were involved. He was out of the hospital in three or four days. His skin type caused his scars to grow. Scars covered his face and neck. Before his accident, he loved school and was doing very well, but children at school made fun of him, and he would hide in the house so that he would miss the school bus. They knew my parents had no car to take him. They moved, but it was just as bad in the next school. They lived out in the country. One day on the bus, a kid was calling him scarface and taunting him until he started crying. My sister, Rosie, was probably thirteen at the time, followed the boy off the bus and into his home and told his mother what he did. She said, "Our mom spanks us if we make fun of anyone, and if you don't spank him, I will." His mother spanked him, and my sister walked home. Eventually, he got to have surgery, which helped, and he went on to have a good life. He had worked on his testimony for a few years there. Then in his early thirties, he swallowed a fishbone while eating fish. He didn't realize it, or it went down, and he figured it would pass through. He started having diarrhea issues that lasted for two weeks. He was on the big truck all week, so he went to the doctor when he got home. They gave him medicines, but it didn't clear up. The third week I think he was in Kentucky. He was three or four hours away from home. He called his wife and said that he was in so much pain that he couldn't drive. He told her to bring a driver for the truck and come get him and take him back to our hospital. He said he didn't want to be in a hospital away from home. We had a sister who was an RN at our local hospital. We all trusted her word. His wife brought him back. He was admitted and in lots of pain. They ruled out appendicitis, and after three days of no improvement, they went in and took out twelve inches of his intestine that was about to be gangrene. After two or three weeks at home resting, his incision opened and was draining. He stayed with our sister Rosie who was an RN, and she cared for him. Then he came and spent two weeks at my house. We all loved it, my kids especially. He visited family through his three-month recovery. At some point afterward, he was driving around the curve on a two-lane road not far from where he lived. A tree had fallen completely across the road. He couldn't stop in time. He said, a hand pushed him over in the seat. He put his arm over his head as the entire top of the car was peeled off. He had two or three small scratches on his arm, but he walked away safe. Sometime later, he rounded a curve on a wet road again. He was in an old van. If he had been in a car, he would have been a goner. He slid up and under a dump truck and knocked it off the road. Once again, he said, a hand shoved him over in the seat. He sustained a lot of damage to his left arm and knee. They had to put cadaver bone and titanium in his arm. He healed so well. His doctor called him his miracle patient. It was coming up on bow season. He loved to deer hunt. He asked the doctor if he would be able to use his arm to go bow hunting. The doctor said not this year, but when the doctor told him he could start using his arm a little, he started pulling that bow a little each day. On the first day of bow season, he went hunting. He told his doctor that his God was a good healer and answered prayers. They were in agreement. His faith grew a lot through that experience. We spent a lot of Sundays together. He, his lovely wife Carole, our sister Nora and I would meet for an early breakfast and then go visit our cousin who was in prison. Our cousin was like a little brother to us. He was incarcerated for twenty years, so we did a lot of life on those Sundays. We all grew in Jesus, including our cousin. When my baby brother Terry and baby sister Nora passed, my oldest brother and his lovely wife went to the prison together and grew closer through those Sundays. Baby brother died of a blood clot to the heart at the age of forty-four, but he left behind a powerful witness and great testimony of someone who loved Jesus and others. He was well-loved by most of all who met him. He was kind and thoughtful. His wife, daughters, and grandchildren adored him. He was a super Pawpaw.

"Wherefore thou art great, O Lord God: for there is none like thee, neither is there any God beside thee, according to all that we have heard with our ears" (2 Samuel 7:22 KJV).

"Blessed be the Lord, who daily loadeth us with benefits, even the God of our salvation. Selah" (Psalm 68:19 KJV).

HEARING THE FATHER'S VOICE

My baby brother died at age forty-four with a blood clot to the heart. He was a truck driver and didn't get out to walk often enough. My oldest brother talked to him about it. He also is a truck driver. He realized something was wrong after eight hours of antacids. He drove himself to an emergency room where he passed away while talking to his wife on the phone. It was so sudden. I was stopping for gas when I got the call. It was a new gas station, and the pay-at-the-pump wasn't set up yet, so I had to go in to pay. I was crying and in shock. There was a beautiful, slender black lady who waited on me and she asked me what was wrong, and I told her that my baby brother had just died. She laid her body across the counter and held and comforted me, and got me some tissues. I went back to thank her two weeks later, and she was there. I told her that she was the arms of Jesus to me that day and His voice of comfort. I went back many times, and I never saw her again, but I'm so thankful that she was there for me that day. For years, I have said that before I die, I want to see someone raised from the dead. I had heard the pastor where I was attending church say that he also wanted to see someone raised from the dead. My baby brother died in Chicago, and we had to wait for an autopsy before his body could be released and brought back to Georgia. I asked my pastor to agree with me that God would raise my brother from the dead. He prayed and agreed with me. We only had one day of visitation. Then the funeral was the next day. On the night of his visitation, I made sure I was the last one to leave. I went into the room. I walked over to the casket and put my hand on his arm, and I said, "Lord. I know he has had an autopsy and has had skin, bone, and organs harvested, but Lazarus was dead for four days, and I believe you can do it." My eyes were closed, and my brother's arm moved under my hand, and my eyes flew open. I was staring into his face waiting for his eyes to open and for him to sit up and speak. The Lord said to me, "Vickie, I can do what you are asking me to do, but it is better for him that I don't." I said, "Lord, his work isn't finished. He was just really growing in the Lord and witnessing." The Lord said to me, "You will see his work finished and soon." I said, "Lord, You didn't have to acknowledge me, but You did, and I thank You." And I did see my brother's work finished. He loved his wife. She had some sickness and disability and depended on him. I think God had to move him out of the way to get closer to her. She and their kids and grandkids did all get closer to God. They wanted to make sure they were all together in eternity. I have not yet seen anyone raised from the dead, but a beautiful resurrection happens inside of us when we die to the old man, and Jesus Christ comes alive in us through the power of the Holy Spirit.

> Do not be anxious or worried about anything, but in everything [every circumstance and situation] by prayer and petition with thanksgiving, continue to make your [specific] requests known to God.

And the peace of God [that peace which reassures the heart, that peace] which transcends all understanding, [that peace which] stands guard over your hearts and your minds in Christ Jesus [is yours].

Philippians 4:6-7 (AMP)

But to each one is given the manifestation of the Spirit [the spiritual illumination and the enabling of the Holy Spirit] for the common good. To one is given through the [Holy] Spirit [the power to speak] the message of wisdom, and to another [the power to express] the word of knowledge and understanding according to the same Spirit; to another [wonder-working] faith [is given] by the same [Holy] Spirit, and to another the [extraordinary] gifts of healings by the one Spirit.

1 Corinthians 12:7-9 (AMP)

THE FRAGRANCE OF HEAVEN

Three weeks after my baby brother died, I was house-sitting for a couple and caring for their dogs. That night I left to go to my third shift job at a carpet mill. I went out and opened the locked door, and as soon as I opened the door, I was breathing in the most beautiful fragrance I have ever smelled in my life. I started thinking, "How did someone get in here? There must have been a bouquet that's been put in here" (although I've never smelled a flower bouquet that smelled that good). I was just deep breathing it in. I couldn't get enough. It was thick with a presence all the way to work. I loved it. I didn't feel a presence there, but the fragrance was sweeter than anything we have here. I couldn't wait to get back to my Jeep the next morning when I finished work. I wondered if the fragrance was still there. Not a trace. I was disappointed, but I knew I had been given a gift. I pray that my life is a sweet fragrance to the Lord, who has been so good to me.

> "Let the words of my mouth, and the meditation of my heart, be acceptable in thy sight, O Lord, my strength, and my redeemer" (Psalm 19:14 KJV).

"O give thanks unto the Lord; call upon his name: make known his deeds among the people. Sing unto him, sing psalms unto him: talk ye of all his wondrous works" (Psalm 105:1-2 KJV).

YEA, THOUGH I WALK THROUGH THE VALLEY OF THE SHADOW OF DEATH

When my baby sister was going through lung cancer, she took ten radiation treatments. On the last treatment, they burned her chest really bad. They gave her pain medicine and cream to put on it, but it didn't seem to help. I was buying groceries and was in the produce department, and she called and said, "Vickie, please pray. The pain is more than I can take, and the pain medicines are not helping." I began to pray out loud, with tears streaming down my face. I said, "God, my sister needs help. I have heard all of my life there was a verse in the Bible that would take the pain out of a burn. I don't know it, but I know You and Your word, and I'm asking You to perform Your word and take the pain out." And He did. That is our amazing God. The *I Am* of our need will answer.

My baby sister never stopped smoking and did not get her healing. She battled cancer for five years before going to see Jesus. She told me that she read the entire Bible over three times. She loved to pray for people. She told me over and over how she thanked God for her cancer and how it had changed her life, but she also changed a lot of other lives as she went through it. I thank God for her husband, who cared for her so faithfully over those five years. The night she passed away, I left her house after the funeral home took her body, and I went to go tell her twenty-four-year-old son. He lived in another county. I think it was about 5:30 in the morning. It was dark. I went and opened the gate, went through his yard, and knocked on his door. I knew he had a vicious dog, but it never entered my mind. I was just dreading having to tell him that his mother was gone. He opened the door and said, "How did you get through the yard to this door?" I said, "What do you mean?" He said, "Look behind you." There stood his dog. He said that his dad couldn't even come into the yard without him having to go out and hold that dog. He said that no one has ever just walked in there. I told him that God knew that I needed to, and He quieted that dog. I walked back out with no interference from the dog. I'm not a dog whisperer, but Jesus is. The *I Am* who is whatever we need Him to be.

> "I am the Lord, the God of all mankind. Is anything too hard for me?" (Jeremiah 32:27 NIV)

> "If I take the wings of the dawn, If I dwell in the remotest part of the sea, Even there Your hand will lead me, And Your right hand will lay hold of me. If I say, 'Surely the darkness will overwhelm me, And the light around me will be night'" (Psalm 139:9-11 NASB).

OUR NEED, HIS PROVISION

My baby sister, Nora, battled cancer for five years. When the cancer got really bad, she needed medication for pain and her infection that was $400. She didn't have the money. She told me if she didn't get the medicine, that her body would go into withdrawals. She asked me to pray that God would make a way. I cleaned a house for a lady in addition to working my carpet mill job. Our work was down to four days, and I didn't have any extra money. I was barely able to pay my bills. The lady that I cleaned house for was wealthy, but I didn't ask for anything. It was near Christmas, so I knew that she would give me a bonus. The year before, she gave me a $200 bonus, so I thought that that's what she would give me this year, and then I could give that money to my sister, and somehow we would get the rest. When I went to leave after cleaning her house, she gave me a check for $650. I went straight to the bank and cashed it, and took it to my sister for her husband to get her the medication. She didn't want to take it. She said somehow they would pay it back. I said, "No, it's not mine. God sent this to you. I asked Him to provide, and He did." Where she was going for treatment, she was doing experimental chemo plus radiation because she had no insurance. They got her on a program that paid for her medication. After that, her husband was laid off from work and was able to draw unemployment, and it was God's provision that he was there to care for her for the rest of her days. He did an amazing job. She died in his arms and is now with Jesus. She thanked God for her cancer. She said she would have never known Him so well without it. She read the Bible over three times during that time. Our God is an awesome God!

> "And my God shall supply all your need according to His riches in glory by Christ Jesus" (Philippians 4:19 NKJV).

> Surely my soul remembers and is bowed down within me. This I recall to my mind, therefore I have hope. The Lord's loving kindnesses indeed never cease, for His compassions never fail. They are new every morning; Great is Your faithfulness. "The Lord is my portion," says my soul, "Therefore I have hope in Him." The Lord is good to those who wait for Him, to the person who seeks Him. It is good that he waits silently for the salvation of the Lord.
> Lamentations 3:20-26 (NASB)

ANGELS

My sister, Louise, used to always see angels praying when things went wrong, or she would dream of my mom after my mom died. I've never dreamed of my mom, but one day right before a death in the family, I smelled her presence. She loved honeysuckle fragrance, and I do too. We have the vines and bushes here in the south, and for the times they were not in season, I would get her honeysuckle perfume and bath powder. Louise saw angels knelt with heads bowed while praying a couple of nights before her husband died. She felt the death angel in the house, and she prayed and said, "God, please not tonight. Please don't take him tonight. I can't handle it." She heard the door close, and the death angel left. Our Father wanted her to know He answered her prayers. He gave her two more days with her husband. Shortly thereafter, her grandson Charlie was in kindergarten. He had a bad milk allergy. A child next to him spilled his milk, and it got on Charlie, who had a bad reaction and an ambulance ride to the hospital. After it was all over, Louise said to him, "I'm sorry you had to go through that. You must have been very afraid." He said, "No, grandma, I wasn't afraid. There were angels all around me." They took good care of him. Thank you, Father, for answered prayers. Louise had many wonderful stories of God's grace, mercy, and miracles. I can't remember them all. Our stories give hope to others as they see how God brings us through. Our stories need to be told. Share with others what God is doing for you.

> "The LORD your God is with you, the Mighty Warrior who saves. He will take great delight in you; in his love he will no longer rebuke you, but will rejoice over you with singing" (Zephaniah 3:17 NIV).

> "For it is written: 'He will command his angels concerning you to guard you carefully'" (Luke 4:10 NIV).

GOD SHOWS UP WHEN WE LEAST EXPECT

In late 2004, I took over caring for my dad's brother, my Uncle Roy. I think he was eighty-one at the time. He had dementia. My baby brother cared for him several years before my brother's death. He had told me one week before he passed that we needed to put uncle Roy somewhere safe. He said, "With my job, I don't get to see him every day, and he is hiding food. When we prepare food for him, we find it still sitting out uneaten two days later, and often the burners are turned on on the stove with nothing on them, and it's an old house." We had made a plan to discuss what to do when he got back off of his next run in his truck, but a blood clot changed those plans. His return home the next week was in a hearse, so my younger sister and I took Uncle Roy and got him admitted to the hospital and evaluated. We put him in a ward for people with Alzheimer's and dementia. His body was healthy, but he had dementia for probably twenty years. He wore overalls, and we cleaned half of a paper grocery bag of stuff from the pockets. He used to stay with us when I was in first grade and before. He played with all of us kids and carved things out of wood for us. He was always happy, smiling, and joyful. He married when I was probably in first grade. He and his wife had four beautiful children, two boys, and two girls. Uncle Roy had back and foot problems and never worked much. When he lived at my mom and dad's old place, and my baby brother lived next door, he rarely ever went outside. He said his feet were not okay. I was visiting one day, and he waved to a lady across the street who was working in her flower bed. He was just outside of his door. He said, "That's where Myrtle lives. That's my sister." It wasn't. Myrtle had always lived in Tennessee. I said, "I'm glad you're outside today in the sunshine." He said, "I can get out more now. A doctor came here and put new bones in my feet, and I can walk better." Who knows, maybe God sent an angel to heal his feet because he did walk. He had a son in prison at the time, and I got approved and took him to the prison several times to see his son and to church, which he enjoyed. I loved his stories. He did not remember who I was. He remembered the older kids, and he could name every neighbor who lived around him in Tennessee. He told me he bought all of their farms and was moving back to Tennessee. If he saw on the news that a big utility company sold, he thought he could buy it and was sure he did. He was always very happy. He would say, "Oh, there's my buddy," or "There's my angel," when I would come to see him. One day he would tell me he was a Texas ranger, sometimes a doctor. One day, he told me he was a postal worker and made $50,000 a week. He was a joy. He would sing with the radio when we were in the car sometimes. At Christmas, I asked the nursing home if I could bring him a tiny one-and-a-half foot tree to go on his dresser. They said as long as it had no lights or break-able ornaments, so I got him a little tree, some cute wood, and plastic ornaments, and I found a string of nine-foot-long plastic gold medallions. His tree was pretty. Two weeks later, I went to get him to take him to see his son in prison. He was in the restroom, and his tree was empty with ornaments scattered everywhere. I didn't see the string of medallions anywhere. I picked up the rest and put it back together, and we went to the prison. When I was helping him out of the Jeep and into a wheelchair (it was too long of a walk for him into the prison), I noticed a big bulge in his pocket and said, "Uncle Roy, what is in your pocket? We have to leave it in the Jeep." He pulled out that nine-foot strand of medallions and said, "These are my badges. You know I'm a Texas ranger policeman," and I can't remember it all, but he was a hoot. He ended up with pneumonia that winter and then fell and broke his hip later. When I got to the hospital, he smiled so big and said, "Mom is here." I said, "Really, I didn't get to see her yet." He said, "Yep, she's here." I thought he was about to go and leave to see her, but I think he lived about six months after he broke his hip. I think that he was afraid to get up. He quit walking and died at age eighty-three. I loved his smiling face and sweet attitude.

> "A merry heart doeth good like a medi-
> cine: but a broken spirit drieth the bones"
> (Proverbs 17:22 KJV).

> "But the fruit of the spirit is love, joy,
> peace, forbearance, kindness, goodness,
> faithfulness, gentleness and self-con-
> trol. Against such things there is no law"
> (Galatians 5:22-23 NIV).

EVER LEARNING

My brother, Robert, told me a story about our Aunt Pauline, who was my mother's sister. She was married to my dad's brother. My brother, Robert, was in church at that point, but there was not a real commitment in his life, and those years he was in and out. He had a serious drinking problem and a pride problem. He was always right. He had said something about Aunt Pauline speaking in tongues and praying for people, and I think it was that he didn't think she should. One time he got sick and had no money to go to the doctor and no insurance. His ears were infected and hurt so bad that when he tried to lay down, he couldn't stand to touch his ears to the pillow. The Lord told him to go get Aunt Pauline to pray for him. In shame, he went. He knocked on the door. Uncle Dot answered, and he said, "Get on in here. She's in the kitchen waiting for you." He went in and sat on a chair. He said she grabbed him on each side of his head, and she began to pray and speak in tongues. He thought she would pull his ears off. He said the pain was terrible. When she finished, she told him to go home and go to bed. He did, and he slept through the night and woke up fine the next morning. Before he finally committed his way to God, he would drink and drive and not take care of his responsibilities. He had gotten so many DUIs he knew he couldn't get any more, so he would find him a place in the woods to drink and pass out or just sleep it off before he went home. He was in the woods one day drinking, and he said that God spoke to him and said, "Robert, I'm tired of fooling with you. You lay it down, or I'm done." I'm not sure what God meant—I'm going to take you on and your work not get done, or I will turn you over to a reprobate mind. I can't speak for God, but Robert said God said enough, and he took God at His word. He asked God to help him, and he laid the drinking at the feet of Jesus and left it there, but his temper stayed a while. He was always a fighter. He would fight anyone over anything, but he asked God to take it. One day, he got into an argument with a neighbor, and the man hit him and knocked him down. Robert held up his hands and said, "Brother, I'm sorry I offended you, but I will not fight you." He got up, and the man knocked him down again. He said he knew he was delivered because he had no desire to hit him back. When my brother passed, he was walking with God very close and loving everyone. His favorite song, and one that he sang well, was *Amazing Grace (My Chains are Gone)*. His second favorite was *The Old Man is Dead*.

"Since they thought it foolish to acknowledge God, he abandoned them to their foolish thinking and let them do things that should never be done" (Romans 1:28 NLT).

"'For I know the plans I have for you,' declares the LORD, 'plans to prosper you and not to harm you, plans to give you hope and a future'" (Jeremiah 29:11 NIV).

"And I am certain that God, who began the good work within you, will continue his work until it is finally finished on the day when Christ Jesus returns" (Philippians 1:6 NLT).

PREPARED

Three years ago, one of my cousins moved back to our area and asked if I would go take him to see my brother Robert. It had been a while since they had seen each other. It was Sunday afternoon. We drove over after church and lunch. The two of them were laughing at an old TV show and making lots of noise. My phone rang, and I walked outside to answer. It was my sister Barbara. Sometimes when a loved one is going to pass, funeral songs will start playing in my head. My sister Barbara will have a bird get in her house. I guess they come in the doggy door. Well, I was standing in Robert's yard, and she said, "Sis, my bird came, and God told me to call and prepare you that one of ours that is close is going home to heaven soon." I always take food to the funeral home and try to feed everybody. We prayed, and the next morning my brother Robert got up and was walking through his hallway and died of a heart attack. I called my sister Barbara. We don't live in the same town. Later that afternoon, she called me back and said, "Sis, another one is going. My bird came back, and God told me to tell you one more was going." Sure enough, his granddaughter, who was states away, was in a bad car accident and went to be with Jesus that afternoon. Sometimes God prepares us. If we are forewarned and prepared, we are more able to help others.

"Precious in the sight of the LORD is the death of his faithful servants" (Psalm 116:15 NIV).

"However, as it is written: What no eye has seen, what no ear has heard, and what no human mind has conceived—the things God has prepared for those who love him" (1 Corinthians 2:9 NIV).

CONFIRMATION FROM GOD

About thirty years ago, I was working a food service job at our hospital. I worked with a young lady who had a miscarriage with her first baby and was five months pregnant with her second baby. The doctor told her they thought something was wrong with the baby. They drew fluid and tested it to check for birth defects. I was off work the day she had the test, so when I came back to work, I started to ask her about it, and my coworkers were shaking their heads no at me, not to say anything. One of them took me aside and told me that the doctor told her that she needed to abort the baby, that it wasn't going to be okay, and that she shouldn't deliver it. I heard God tell me to tell her that her baby was going to be okay. I was afraid to tell her. I thought, "What if this is Satan putting this thought in my mind to destroy my testimony?" We had a walk-in vegetable cooler. I went inside the cooler and said, "God, I need to know if that was You talking to me." I felt a surge of energy/power go through from the top of my head through my body. He said, "Now, go tell her what I said." I did, and she received the word. She carried her baby to full term and birthed a beautiful, healthy baby girl who was completely okay. The God I serve speaks to His children and wants to hear their voice. If you think that you've never heard Him, ask. Ask Him to speak to you. He answers prayer. We don't always get the answer we want or when we want it. He is a wise Father. I am thankful He didn't answer some of those prayers that I prayed and that some were answered at the right time. He sees the future. He knows when the right time is. One of the prayers that I have prayed for over forty years is being answered now.

> "Teach me to do your will, for you are my God. May your gracious Spirit lead me forward on a firm footing" (Psalm 143:10 NLT).

> "But joyful are those who have the God of Israel as their helper, whose hope is in the Lord their God" (Psalm 146:5 NLT).

LOVE ONE ANOTHER AS I HAVE LOVED YOU

I was working a job in my mid-to-late thirties, and I worked with a girl who could get under my skin in a New York minute. Our personalities collided easily. We are around people daily where we go to church, where we work, where we play, who are very different from us. The Word didn't say love them if they are like you or if you approve of their lifestyle or how they talk. I just had a struggle with her, her attitude, work ethic, etc. One day the Lord spoke very clearly to me and said, "You are ruining your testimony with this attitude you have towards her, and if you cannot love her like you love everyone else, you are not right with me." I got down on my knees and repented and asked God's help with the situation and asked Him to put a love in my heart for her, and He did. Now thirty years later, if I see her or think of her, they are loving, happy thoughts. I would love to sit down with her now and see where the Lord has taken us both through the years. Probably six months after the Lord helped me get rid of my bad attitude toward her, my first sibling died. I was called and told at work. I went to the bathroom and fell apart. A lady from another department asked me how she could help and who she could get for me. That girl that I had the problem with was the first one who came to my mind.

She was there in an instant. She comforted me and helped me so very much. She is counted as precious to me today. We have an enemy who tries to divide us, but the Creator of our soul desires love and unity among the brethren.

"If it is possible, as far as it depends on you, live at peace with everyone" (Romans 12:18 NIV).

"Continually pursue peace with everyone, and the sanctification without which no one will [ever] see the Lord" (Hebrews 12:14 AMP).

"Beloved, let us [unselfishly] love and seek the best for one another, for love is from God; and everyone who loves [others] is born of God and knows God [through personal experience]" (1 John 4:7 AMP).

Love endures with patience and serenity, love is kind and thoughtful, and is not jealous or envious; love does not brag and is not proud or arrogant. It is not rude; it is not self-seeking, it is not provoked [nor overly sensitive and easily angered]; it does not take into account a wrong endured. It does not rejoice at injustice, but rejoices with the truth [when right and truth prevail]. Love bears all things [regardless of what comes], believes all things [looking for the best in each one], hopes all things [remaining steadfast during difficult times], endures all things [without weakening].

1 Corinthians 13:4-7 (AMP)

LISTEN AND LEARN

I was on a job years ago that God was trying to get me to leave, and I wasn't getting it. I was afraid to quit then. It was right before the holidays. God gave me a dream of me walking through a parking lot and someone coming up from behind and backstabbing me. He showed me two people that I worked with at that time and told me to quit. I did. I had not found a job yet, and they called me three times, begging me to come back to work and making me promises. I didn't ask God about it. I went back. When we made it through the holiday crunch, I took two days off to go to a youth conference. I came home to a FedEx letter that said, "We now accept your letter of resignation." Those two people stabbed me literally in the back by persuading me to come back and then not keeping their promises and then saying, now we accept your resignation and booting me out the door, but it was a God thing. He was saying, "If you won't listen, you're going to learn this the hard way." He did take care of my kids and me, and I try to listen better these days. He's talking and trying to work all things together for our good (Romans 8:28), but we've got to listen. If you hear something and you are unsure, ask God for confirmation.

"In their hearts, humans plan their course, but the Lord establishes their steps" (Proverbs 16:9 NIV).

"Yes, my soul, find rest in God; my hope comes from him" (Psalm 62:5 NIV).

STUBBORNNESS AND WILL

I worked with a woman many years ago who was one of my supervisors. She was very stubborn and mean-spirited. You know, like me and many others of us were before Jesus came to live in our hearts, and sometimes even afterward, those bad attitudes sneak in on us. Anyway, she was very proud when her daughter married. It was a beautiful wedding. All seemed great until many months, or maybe a year later, her daughter told her that she was going to be a grandmother. She was furious. She was only thirty-nine. She thought she was too young. She and her husband were not ready to be grandparents. She didn't like it. She felt they should have waited a few years. I used to tell people, "She's mean alright, but she just needs Jesus." I did pray for her to find Him. I can't remember if the baby was born before I left that job, but of course, they loved him. His name was Will. I'm sure they thought, like all of us, that they had the most gorgeous grandchild of all. I would see her from time to time out somewhere, and we would say hello but not really talk. Then after several years, we saw each other again out somewhere and had a conversation. I immediately saw a change in her life. I think she said her grandson was three when he told them about Jesus and asked them to go to church. I believe it was on Easter. They both surrendered their hearts and their lives to Jesus Christ. Praise God for a little Will.

"But God demonstrates his own love for us in this: While we were still sinners, Christ died for us" (Romans 5:8 NIV).

"Jesus said, 'Let the little children come to me, and do not hinder them, for the kingdom of heaven belongs to such as these'" (Matthew 19:14 NIV).

OUR GOD SPEAKS,
SOMETIMES OUT LOUD

Years ago, when I worked in the hospital cafeteria, a little lady named Marie came to work with us. I loved her so much. She was such a Godly woman and a hard worker. She was probably about seventy years old when she came. Her mother was in her final years and passed while we worked together. Marie's mom was bedridden, but in her perfect mind and was ninety-six years old when she went home to Jesus. Marie helped care for her, worked full-time, and helped raise a young granddaughter whose dad was in bed with a hurt back most of the time. She told me that at Thanksgiving that year, all three of her boys and their families were at her house. Her husband had passed away already. As they sat down for their Thanksgiving meal, her oldest son sat in his dad's chair, and they all joined hands and prayed. As they finished praying, all of them clearly heard their dad say, "This is the way it should be." She said some days after a really rough day; she would feel her husband sit down on the side of the bed to remind her he was still with her in spirit. Sometimes we connect between heaven and Earth. My sister-in-law recently told me that she feels my brother sitting on the side of the bed sometimes, and he has been in heaven for about two-and-a-half years now.

"Peace I leave with you; my peace I give you. I do not give to you as the world gives. Do not let your hearts be troubled and do not be afraid" (John 14:27 NIV).

ANSWERED PRAYER, ANOTHER LITTLE MARIE STORY

One night after closing the hospital cafeteria, Marie and I were working a few feet apart cleaning our work area. Everyone else was back in the kitchen or back in their prep areas. Marie cried out in pain and grabbed her chest. She was doubled over. I grabbed her in my arms to keep her from falling, and I cried out to God to do something now and I began to pray. In a minute, she was okay. I begged her to go to the emergency room. She said, "No, I'll go to my doctor tomorrow. You know it's my day off." She promised me if I would not say anything that she would be okay and would go to the doctor, but she said, "If you had not prayed Vickie, I would have died." The next morning I felt no peace that she would go to the doctor, and I was worried. I called her doctor and asked them if she had called and made an appointment, and they said no. I heard her say where her oldest son worked, so I called him and told him I was worried about her and what had happened. Her son left work and took her to her doctor. Her doctor didn't do an EKG. Back in those days they didn't have that at their office, but they did do blood work, and he told her and her son that her potassium was so low it was a miracle she had not had a heart attack. She worked many more years after I left there. Then I was shopping one afternoon, and I saw her working at Walmart. She was up on a high ladder getting something off of the top shelf. She had to be about seventy-three years old at that time. She was a joy to know and work with. She was an amazing, wise woman of God who left behind a great legacy.

> "And he said to her, 'Daughter, your faith has made you well. Go in peace. Your suffering is over'" (Mark 5:34 NLT).

A Beautiful Sunrise

I was driving my five-year-old grandson Caiden to preschool one morning, and as we were coming out of the subdivision, the sunrise before us was magnificent. He said to me, "Nana, do you know what that makes me think of? It makes me think of what Jesus did for me on the cross." I was in tears. What a beautiful statement from a five-year-old, and the fact that he understood, wow. Thank you, Jesus.

> "From the rising of the sun to the place where it sets, the name of the Lord is to be praised" (Psalm 113:3 NIV).

Before Caiden was born, my daughter and son-in-law asked me to pick a Biblical middle name for him. I chose Isaiah. I said, "He will be a Word carrier." Isaiah said, "Here I am, Lord, send me." However, I pray that of all my grandchildren, each one of them will be Word carriers. We were on vacation that year, and we were in a house in Orlando. He was lying on the sofa watching cartoons. I walked into the room, and I said, "There's my little Word carrier." He raised up, looked at me, and said, "That's right, Nana, and I'm going to do it. I'm going to tell people about Jesus." Shortly thereafter, he went through a time where he wouldn't speak to anyone except for me, his mom, and his dad. I said,

"Caiden, you are being rude when someone speaks to you; you need to speak back." He said, "I can't, Nana. I can't make the words come out." It continued for a while, and I began to pray and seek God about it. The Holy Spirit told me that Satan was trying to steal his voice so he could not carry out his calling. He overcame in the name of Jesus.

> "For God has not given us a spirit of fear and timidity, but of power, love, and self-discipline" (2 Timothy 1:7 NLT).

OUR FATHER IS ALWAYS AT WORK

In 2007, I applied for a part-time job at our local mall. It was a holiday position. Our work at the carpet mill was down, and gas prices were way up. My daughter and her husband had a small baby. We all three worked different shifts. I lived with them and watched my grandson during the day and worked third shift at night. They had built me an apartment in their house. They did not want him in daycare, so I took a weekend job because times were hard. The day I got hired, they also hired an eighteen-year-old girl. When I was there, I worked on the sales floor of a department store, keeping it tidy and watching the dressing rooms. The young girl worked at the register. She would come and follow me around the store as I worked my section. I would talk about Jesus and what He was doing in our lives. One day she said, "You talk about Him like He is right here," and she pointed to the space between us, and I said, "He is. Wherever we are, He is. He is ever with us." The boss would come to get her a lot of times and send her back to the register, but she kept coming back. She was hungry to know God more. When I was younger, God gave me a spiritual mom who took me under her arm and taught me so very much about having a relationship with Jesus. I had asked God to give me opportunities to do the same, and He has. This young girl had a boyfriend who was also eighteen. We became good friends. We ate together often at work. They were always trying to feed me. She tried to feed lots of people. The two of them had huge hearts. They both had been in church, and she told me she was saved. The boy never said if he was or not. They had met in school and been dating for three years. He didn't feel comfortable in her church. She didn't feel comfortable in his church. So I said to them, "Well, if you're going to be married someday, you need to find a church together that feels right." So they did. They asked me to go visit their church, and I said I would. They insisted on coming to get me, and it was quite a drive for them. I wonder now if they were worried that I wouldn't come if they didn't come to get me, but I went. Then they took me to lunch and then we came back to my place and were in my apartment just talking when she told her boyfriend to tell me about his dream. He said that he had dreamed that he was sitting on a park bench talking to a man. He said he liked talking to him, and then another man came and got in front of him and wouldn't stop talking. He didn't want to talk to him, and the man on the bench said, "You have to make him stop." so he told him to leave him alone and go away. The man reached out and grabbed his lower leg and burned it. He said when he woke up, his leg was burned. He pulled up his pant leg, and there was a three-inch circle. The hair was burned off, and there were three scratches in that spot. He asked me what I thought that meant. I said, "Jesus was the man on the bench that you enjoyed talking to, and Satan was the one in front of you that wouldn't shut up. They both want you. You need to make a decision." He said, "I choose Jesus." I asked him if he was ready to pray, and he said yes, so I led him in the sinner's prayer. Then he asked me, "What do I do now?" I said,

"When you go to church tonight, tell your pastor that you prayed and accepted Jesus and that you need to be baptized." He did. Both of them were so honest and sincere. She called me that night and told me that he was going to be baptized in two weeks and asked me if I would come, and I said yes, and I did. The girl asked me if I remembered the day that we were both hired, and I said yes. She said, "You finished your paperwork before me and left, and I didn't know who you were, but I did not want you to walk out of that room and leave me." She said, "Today, when you prayed with my boyfriend, I prayed that prayer with you also, and I feel different. I think maybe I just thought I was saved, and I wasn't saved." I said, "Or maybe you just needed a recommitment, but either way, I'm glad you prayed, and you feel renewed." I watched as they were faithful to church and to Christ. They wanted to get married and had little money or family support. The preacher said he would marry them. I baked a wedding cake, and my daughter took some pictures. My daughter-in-law directed the wedding. I was the matron of honor, and I was honored to do it. Their families did not offer much help or support, but the two of them forged ahead and worked hard. When they had their first son, the economy was bad, and the young man couldn't get a good job, so he joined the military so he could provide for his family. I told him, "You are first a soldier of the cross and of Jesus and second an army soldier. You are a mighty man of God and a leader—never be a follower." You lead others by the example of Jesus. We all go through trials and tribulations in this life. None of us are exempt, but these two are wonderful examples of holding on to Jesus and each other, overcoming the past, making a bright future as followers of Jesus, and raising two fine sons to walk in the footsteps of Jesus. It's amazing to watch our Father at work, and He is only beginning. That wonderful young man has answered the call to preach, and I had the privilege of watching him preach his first sermon last week. Their walk of faith is amazing to watch, and they are raising up two fine sons to walk with God up close. I thank my God as I see Him at work in all our lives.

> "I will praise you, LORD, with all my heart; I will tell of all the marvelous things you have done. I will be filled with joy because of you. I will sing praises to your name, O Most High" (Psalm 9:1-2 NLT).

> "The LORD directs the steps of the godly. He delights in every detail of their lives" (Psalm 37:23 NLT).

OUT OF THE MOUTHS OF BABES

I was sitting on my carport one night with my grandsons, Parker and Caiden, and we were all around my little fire pit that my friend Luz gave me. We had toasted hot dogs and then marshmallows and were waiting for the fire to go down before going inside. It was dusk. I can't remember if it was spring or fall. Parker was about three, and Caiden was about seven. They had gone on a campout with friends from church not long before this, and Parker had learned the song kumbaya. He got out of his chair and started going around the campfire with his hands in the air, singing kumbaya and telling me, "Nana, this is how you praise God." I looked over, and Caiden had his hands up, and his eyes closed in prayer. I was overwhelmed with joy. Parker began to make up songs and sing to Jesus, and he said again, "Nana, this is how you praise God." I'm so thankful that my grandchildren have heard the gospel, believe it, and are growing in it. I'm thankful my children and their mates take them to church and teach them the Word of God. Parents, grandparents—we are bringing up the next generation. Take time for God. Make Him a priority. Teach your family to do the same.

"Start children off on the way they should go, and even when they are old they will not turn from it" (Proverbs 22:6 NIV).

Oh, that their hearts would be inclined to fear me and keep all my commands always, so that it might go well with them and their children forever! "Go, tell them to return to their tents. But you stay here with me so that I may give you all the commands, decrees and laws you are to teach them to follow in the land I am giving them to possess." So be careful to do what the Lord your God has commanded you; do not turn aside to the right or to the left. Walk in obedience to all that the Lord your God has commanded you, so that you may live and prosper and prolong your days in the land that you will possess.

Deuteronomy 5:29-33 (NIV)

Teach them to your children, talking about them when you sit at home and when you walk along the road, when you lie down and when you get up. Write them on the doorframes of your houses and on your gates, so that your days and the days of your children may be many in the land the Lord swore to give your ancestors, as many as the days that the heavens are above the earth. If you carefully observe all these commands I am giving you to follow—to love the Lord your God, to walk in obedience to him and to hold fast to him.

Deuteronomy 11:19-22 (NIV)

LIFE LESSON

My granddaughter, who had just turned sixteen at the time, was coming down their staircase with her little brother, who was about to turn three. She saw him as he tried to come down the stairs carrying one hand and an armful of matchbox cars. She said, "Here, let me put your cars in my big hand and carry them." It was at that moment that she had one of those God moments of how many times we try to carry a heavy load in life instead of putting it in God's larger, more capable hands. I was so proud of her as she related that story. Our Father, through the power of the Holy Spirit, is always looking out for us, waiting for us to ask for His help. Life is less complicated when we give each day to Him at the beginning and ask for His strength and help as we go through each day, and then take time to thank Him at the end of it as we pray for a safe and good night's rest. Thank you, Father God, our Lord and Savior Jesus Christ, and sweet Holy Spirit who helps me 24/7.

> "Cast all your anxiety on him because he cares for you" (1 Peter 5:7 NIV).

> "My command is this: Love each other as I have loved you" (John 15:12 NIV).

SURPRISED BY GOD

A young friend of mine that I work with was expecting his first child when I met him. He was a little disappointed that it was going to be a girl instead of a boy, so I got him a baby bib trimmed in pink that said "Daddy's Girl," which brought a big smile to his face. I think she was three when they decided to have another baby. As soon as they told everyone that his wife was expecting, they lost the baby. They were heartbroken. Months went by, and they decided to try again. When they found out that she was pregnant again, they decided not to tell anyone until she got past her first trimester. I was working his shift one night, and we talked. We each asked about each other's families—just small talk. An hour or so later, I passed him in a walkway, we nodded, and God said to me, "His wife is expecting." A little while later, he brought me some paperwork, and I looked at him and said, "Is there anything that you are not telling me?" He said, "No." I said, "Are you sure?" He said, "I can't think of anything." I looked him in the eye and asked, "Is your wife expecting a baby?" He looked bewildered and said nothing for a couple of minutes, then he asked, "How do you know? We haven't told anyone." I told him that God told me and that I thought it was going to be the boy he had been wanting. He said, "Really?" I asked him if they had picked out any names. He told me a first and middle name for a boy. I heard the Holy Spirit say,

"That's not his name." I said, "I can't tell him that." I didn't say anything about the name. In a little while, he was back again with paperwork and said that he had been thinking about Isaac as his name. I felt tingles go all over my body and the Holy Spirit said, "That's his name." I told him what the Holy Spirit said, and that's what they named him. I couldn't understand why the Holy Spirit told me all that. I didn't realize until months later, and I told him that God wanted him to know that the baby was going to be born, so he gave him a name and a confirmation. That's our God. We are His disciples when we give our hearts to Him and live for Him.

> "So is my word that goes out from my mouth: It will not return to me empty, but will accomplish what I desire and achieve the purpose for which I sent it" (Isaiah 55:11 NIV).

> "And the disciples went everywhere and preached, and the Lord worked through them, confirming what they said by many miraculous signs" (Mark 16:20 NLT).

PRAYER FOR LUZ'S GRANDDAUGHTER'S FEVER

While I was at work one night, my friend Luz called down to my work area and asked me to pray. Her daughter was expecting a baby and something was wrong. She was about six months along. Her husband rushed her to the hospital. We were in North Georgia, and her daughter was in Miami, Florida. My friend Luz was very worried. We prayed together, and when I went on break, she told me that she was in the break room praying, and as she lifted her eyes up off of her arms, she saw a huge angel holding a sleeping little girl. She said, "What does that mean, Vickie? I said, "It means that God has answered our prayers. Your daughter is sleeping. She is fine." Sure enough, her daughter and granddaughter were both fine. Months later, when the baby was about six months old, she got sick and had a very high fever. My mind went to the scripture where Jesus rebuked the fever, and it left. So as I prayed and rebuked the fever, our heavenly Father took the fever away. Luz's daughter called back in minutes and told us that it was gone. Praise God.

> "Then Jesus got up and left the synagogue and went to Simon's (Peter's) house. Now Simon's mother-in-law was suffering

from a high fever, and they asked Him to help her" (Luke 4:38).

"And the prayer of faith will restore the one who is sick, and the Lord will raise him up; and if he has committed sins, he will be forgiven" (James 5:15 NASB).

AT THE RIGHT PLACE AT THE RIGHT TIME

One night our boss was watching as a co-worker was cleaning a steamer. The guy came to the door of the steamer to cool off, and he was talking to the boss. The boss looked down and saw blood coming from under the door. He said, "Man, where are you bleeding?" The guy didn't know he was bleeding. He looked and saw that it was coming from a small cut on his wrist. He didn't remember that he was on a blood thinner. He took several medications. As the boss took him to the office, I began to pray Ezekiel 16:6 three times, and the bleeding stopped. The nurse asked the boss how he stopped the bleeding because he was on a blood thinner. I wasn't there to tell her how, but I did tell the boss.

> "And my God will meet all your needs according to the riches of his glory in Christ Jesus" (Philippians 4:19 NIV).

> "Then I passed by and saw you kicking about in your blood, and as you lay there in your blood I said to you, 'Live!'" (Ezekiel 16:6 NIV) (Pray that verse 3 times in faith believing)

FREEDOM INSIDE PRISON WALLS

I volunteer with a women's prison ministry, and one Saturday, a young woman told me she was so glad when she got caught in her crime, which she didn't name. She just said it felt so good and freeing when it all came out, and she didn't have to try to hide what she was doing and live a double life anymore. How many of us need to confess some things to God and others so we can feel that freedom and not have to hide or feel the shame of it anymore? Our Father knows, and He still loves us. Satan whispers, "What will they say if they know? What will people think of you?" It doesn't matter. If they already love you, then they should continue to love you. Love and forgiveness go hand-in-hand. Don't let Satan hold you under with a secret. Truths need to be told, and the sooner, the better.

> "Each time he said, 'My grace is all you need. My power works best in weakness.' So now I am glad to boast about my weaknesses so that the power of Christ can work through me" (2 Corinthians 12:9 NLT).

"Then you will experience God's peace, which exceeds anything we can understand. His peace will guard your hearts and minds as you live in Christ Jesus" (Philippians 4:7 NLT).

Receiving Freedom in Prison

I met a lady in a women's prison as I was volunteering with a ministry. I think sometimes we receive much more than we give. As we go in to worship, I see the love of God in that place so precious and overflowing. I look in the faces I've never seen before, and I feel overwhelming love for them. I see Jesus show up and bring freedom. I met a lady named Joy, and joy bubbles out of her along with love, peace, and freedom, although she is in prison. She said she went to the prison ministry weekend for one reason only. She heard they were serving red velvet cake, and she wanted some. She looked at me so full of peace and joy and said, "You know what I got? I got the red velvet blood of Jesus all over me!" Praise God. What a testimony. I love it, and I love her. Another lady prayed and forgave her mother. She had lived with the unforgiveness for forty-nine years. What a burden be lifted off of her. Whatever you are going through, whatever you face, we have a loving, heavenly Father holding out His arms saying, put it on Me, and I will carry it. I absolutely love the 23rd Psalm, "He leads me beside the still waters." What a relief! I was in troubled waters for too many years.

"Come to me, all you who are weary and burdened, and I will give you rest" (Matthew 11:28 NIV).

And may you have the power to understand, as all God's people should, how wide, how long, how high, and how deep his love is. May you experience the love of Christ, though it is too great to understand fully. Then you will be made complete with all the fullness of life and power that comes from God.

Ephesians 3:18-19 (NLT)

PRAYING FOR AN AGNOSTIC

Before I had my two knee surgeries, I used to go to a local assisted living and speak on Wednesdays. A young man at my church had opened that door. My two older sisters, my two aunts, and I would go sing, bring a message, and just spend time with them. We loved it. One day after the message and time together, the young man from my church said, "Vickie, I want you to come back here with me and meet a lady and pray for her." I said okay, and as we were walking back to her room, he told me that she was an agnostic. I had never prayed with one of those before. I asked God to give me the words to say so that I would not offend her or close the door to visit. She was such a beautiful and gracious woman. I assumed her to be in her 70s. He introduced us and asked her how she was doing. We exchanged pleasantries, and I asked if I could pray with her, and she said yes. I asked if I could touch her hand, and again she said yes, so I took her small hand in mine and prayed blessings over and asked God, her Creator, to come into a close relationship with her. I wished her well, and we left. As days went by, I would pray for her to come into a relationship with Jesus. I asked to see her again, and she had visitors that week, so we couldn't. The next week we went back, and she was sleeping. The young man said,

259

"We can still pray. She's hard of hearing, and it won't disturb her." So we stretched our hands above her body and prayed quietly. I asked God again to come into a relationship with her and to reach all the way down to where she was and make Himself real to her. I said, "Lord, you gave me one minute when I asked." (though I think I got at least three). I said, "Will You come as Jesus and give her one minute and answer whatever is keeping her from You and allow her to come into faith with You." I prayed daily for her. I knew she probably didn't have a lot of time left. They had removed her bed from her room, and she was in a hospital bed the last day I prayed with her. I asked to see her the next week, and the young man said we couldn't do it that day, her family was with her. Something in his voice made me feel that she was leaving very soon. He never gave any details of her health, age, sickness, or anything else. He was very professional, and he was a Christian and didn't want her to pass from this life to the next without Jesus. The next week she passed, and I knew in my spirit without being told. As I was thinking about it and wondering if she made it to heaven, I was at work, and no one was within twenty feet of me, and I felt arms come around me and hug me and tingles all over. I said, "God is it her? Did she make it?" He assured me that yes, she did. I just felt in my spirit that it was her and her spirit remained around me for about thirty minutes or so. I bought a newspaper to read her obituary—a half-page long. She was ninety-eight. A remarkable lady—she and her husband had done amazing things to help others. They had put many kids through college. She had only one child, and he died in infancy, and I thought perhaps that's why she didn't want to trust in our Father. We don't understand those things. It hurts deeply, but praise God they are reunited for all eternity.

"Precious in the sight of the Lord is the death of his faithful servants" (Psalm 116:15 NIV).

ONE MINUTE WITH JESUS

At sixty-four years old, I was watching a Christian program and heard a pastor say that he had one minute with Jesus and that it changed his life, and that he had seen amazing miracles of people who also had one minute with Jesus. He said that God is no respecter of persons, and He will give anybody one minute who will ask, so I asked Him that Thursday morning in October if I could have my one minute with Him. Many people probably asked that day as they watched that program for a minute with Him. I was going to work a week later on a Thursday afternoon and decided to stop and vacuum my car. I normally don't have cash or change, but I did that day, so I decided to vacuum on the way to work. I was vacuuming on the passenger side of the car and stopped to pull the hose where I could throw it over to the other side. There had been no one in sight. When I turned away from the car to pull the hose, there was a man about five feet from me. We were in an area where there are often homeless people. He was clean and in jeans with a backpack and a cap on. He had reddish-brown hair down on his shoulders. He asked me if I could give him two or three dollars. I turned my back on him and was getting money out of my wallet. When I turned back around, he was about two feet from me. I gave him the money, but I don't remember putting it in his hand or seeing his hand, but I didn't have it anymore. I had lived as a single woman for over twenty years and was always telling people that I was hug-deficient. I would tell my brothers to hug me twice. He pulled me into his arms and hugged me when I gave him the money, and as naturally as taking the next breath, I put my arms around his neck. He hugged me to the depth of my soul, and I've never felt hug deficient since then. When he hugged me, I said to him, "God bless you, brother," and he said, "and God bless you," and he turned me loose and backed away. As he backed away, he did something to me that I do to people all the time—he pointed at me and said, "If I don't see you again here, I'll see you there," and he pointed up. As I turned back around to my car to vacuum, I said to him, "Amen," and immediately I realized something wasn't right. When he hugged me, I never felt flesh and bone, just pure softness. So I immediately turned back around, and he was gone. There was no way he could have gotten anywhere out of my sight that quick. There was nowhere for him to have gone. I was overwhelmed because I realized that I had just gotten my one minute. The day I asked for my one minute, the pastor was saying that people ask for all types of healing and things. What I had asked for was more witnessing opportunities so I could share Him with others, and as I tell this story, that is what I am doing. He says we have not because we ask not, *so ask*.

> "You have not because you ask not" (James 4:2).

> You have searched me, Lord, and you know me. You know when I sit and when I rise; you perceive my thoughts from afar. You discern my going out and my lying down; you are familiar with all my

ways. Before a word is on my tongue you, Lord, know it completely. You hem me in behind and before, and you lay your hand upon me. Such knowledge is too wonderful for me, too lofty for me to attain. Where can I go from your Spirit? Where can I flee from your presence? If I go up to the heavens, you are there; if I make my bed in the depths, you are there. If I rise on the wings of the dawn, if I settle on the far side of the sea, even there your hand will guide me, your right hand will hold me fast. If I say, "Surely the darkness will hide me and the light become night around me," even the darkness will not be dark to you; the night will shine like the day, for darkness is as light to you. For you created my inmost being; you knit me together in my mother's womb. I praise you because I am fearfully and wonderfully made; your works are wonderful, I know that full well. My frame was not hidden from you when I was made in the secret place, when I was woven together in the depths of the earth. Your eyes saw my unformed body; all the days ordained for me were written in your book before one of them came to be. How precious to me are your thoughts, God! How vast is the sum of them! Were I to count them, they would

outnumber the grains of sand—when I
awake, I am still with you.

Psalm 139:1-18 (NIV)

A DEBORAH STORY— TWO MIRACLES

In 2006, my grandson, Caiden, was born. It was my daughter's first child. He was a gorgeous baby (eight and 1/2 lbs of blessing). At birth, they detected a heart murmur. The pediatrician made an appointment with a cardiologist three months out and told them with each visit, they still heard the heart murmur and not to miss the appointment. He also had an umbilical hernia. One week before the cardiologist appointment, my friend Deborah called and said that she had a dream the night before. In the dream, she was laying hands on people everywhere, and God was healing them. She said that she laid hands on baby Caiden and God healed him. She said she woke up exhausted and wet with sweat like she had run a marathon. The next day, Caiden's belly button was perfect. Now at fourteen years old, he still has a perfect beautiful belly button and a healthy heart. When my daughter and her husband took him to the cardiologist at three months old, they ran all the different tests (x-ray, ultrasound, EKG). Then the cardiologist looked at them a little irritated and said, "I don't know why they sent you here; there's nothing wrong with his heart." I was telling one of my brothers the story, and he said to me, "God took her in the spirit to all of those people she prayed for. It wasn't a dream. She was there. That's why she was exhausted and sweating so bad." I believe that, though I've never experienced it. Our God is a mighty, miracle-working God, every day. We don't always get the miracles we pray for. Why I don't know, but someone will receive a miracle today. It could be you. Ask.

> "And God has placed in the church first of all apostles, second prophets, third teachers, then miracles, then gifts of healing, of helping, of guidance, and of different kinds of tongues" (1 Corinthians 12:28 NIV).

> "'If you can?' said Jesus. 'Everything is possible for one who believes'" (Mark 9:23 NIV).

Prayer Closet

I have a precious friend, who is like a daughter to me, who has fought some fierce battles and has gone through extreme physical and emotional pain. She has a beautiful heart for God and a strong faith. She went through a time of needing a job. It was getting down to the wire. It needed to happen soon. She emptied most of everything out of her closet and made a prayer closet. She spent two days in it, praying for God to move on her behalf. She went to bed, and when she woke up the next morning, Father God told her the name of the company that she had never thought to apply to, and it was closer to her home than the other places she had worked. When she applied, they were ready for her and offered her a job with a larger salary than she had ever dreamed. Our God can open doors we cannot imagine. Once again, my life verse—Romans 8:28, and we know all things work together for good to those who love God and are called according to His purpose.

> "I will bless the Lord at all times, His praise will always be on my lips" (Psalm 34:1 CSB).

> "Do not be anxious about anything, but in every situation, by prayer and petition,

with thanksgiving, present your requests to God" (Philippians 4:6 NIV).

"But when you pray, go into your room, close the door and pray to your Father, who is unseen. Then your Father, who sees what is done in secret, will reward you" (Matthew 6:6 NIV).

A DARK NIGHT
OF THE SOUL

Sometimes we go through big battles, and we don't know how we are going to make it. We all need our brothers and sisters of the faith—our prayer warriors. We went through a terrible battle a few years ago in our family. Two different prayer warriors saw the same vision of angels with wings touching, surrounding the one in the family that was in danger. One of them said the angels were dancing like ceremonial dancing around him. Both said the ground was fiery hot, and they knew he would make it because the angels were there. He had tried to kill himself. A paramedic told him that he should be dead. God has a purpose for you. He has led many to Christ in the midst of the battle. God has worked so much good through the tragedy and pain that we all as a family endured. God is faithful. We are loved. The joy of what God has done surpasses the pain of the battle. Our God is an awesome God.

> Blessed be the God and Father of our Lord Jesus Christ, who according to His great mercy has caused us to be born again to a living hope through the resurrection of Jesus Christ from the dead, to

obtain an inheritance which is imperishable and undefiled and will not fade away, reserved in heaven for you, who are protected by the power of God through faith for a salvation ready to be revealed in the last time. In this you greatly rejoice, even though now for a little while, if necessary, you have been distressed by various trials, so that the proof of your faith, being more precious than gold which is perishable, even though tested by fire, may be found to result in praise and glory and honor at the revelation of Jesus Christ.

1 Peter 1:3-7 (NASB)

My Neighbor, My Friend, My Sister, My Prayer Warrior

An amazing, beautiful young lady with a beautiful little girl moved into the duplex beside me. She was a struggling single mom with lots of troubles. She knew God but didn't yet know who she was in Him. As we began to talk and get to know each other, we prayed a lot together and for one another. I was struggling with a bad back and bad knees. She would pray for me, and I would pray for her. I gave her a new study Bible and a daily devotional that helped her to grow, and like me, she soon found that we really need a daily walk with Jesus. She now, four years later, has been places with Jesus I've never dreamed of, and I'm jealous of. We all have different experiences with God. We are all different people. We relate to God and His word differently, and He responds differently to us. She has had numerous out of body spirit walks with Jesus. He has taken her to the seashore, and she has walked on water with Him. She has visions. She looks for Him everywhere and finds Him. She sent me a picture one day of an angel in the clouds and another day a picture of a cross in the clouds. She loves red birds and sees them everywhere. One night she was praying for four people in real need. I was one of them. It was before my knee surgery, and I had torn my meniscus and had bad arthritis in my right knee. As she asked Him to help us, He took her in the spirit to each of our homes and let her see as He prayed for each of us. She came to see if I was better and told me the story. She said, "I didn't know which knee it was, but you were asleep in the recliner right there." She pointed to the one that I slept in and said, "Jesus bowed at your right knee, put both of His hands on it, laid His head on His hands, and prayed for your knee. My knee didn't get healed, and she nor I understood why. After He came and prayed for it, I had a knee repair. Six months passed, and I had to have a knee replacement. During that time, a tragedy happened in my daughter's family. I was home with that knee healing when my family desperately needed me to be there. I was not working the two jobs that I normally did. I understood, and I thanked Him for healing me enough to get by because He saw what was coming. My little prayer warrior amazes me at how she has grown in Jesus. I know that girl can get a prayer through. I've seen her go through so much, as she has me, and we pray together and help each other. She has amazed me so much as I've seen her grow, and I know she is raising another little prayer warrior. I'm so thankful for her. She is a blessing to me and to our Father in heaven. She has such childlike faith in that she just believes. She doesn't try to rationalize God. She sees His word as truth and steps out on it. We all could use some of that kind of Faith. Thank you, Father, for the gift of Kelly and Ahna in my life. If we never experienced any trials in life, we would be spoiled and know nothing of our need for God and what He can do. We would not grow in faith or be able to help others. I am not saying that God creates the trials. We live in a broken world. In Christ, we overcome and can help others.

"Look to the Lord and his strength; seek his face always" (1 Chronicles 16:11 NIV).

"Therefore confess your sins to each other and pray for each other so that you may be healed. The prayer of a righteous person is powerful and effective" (James 5:16 NIV).

"Do not be anxious about anything, but in every situation, by prayer and petition, with thanksgiving, present your requests to God" (Philippians 4:6 NIV).

My Sister Frances

My sister, Frances, is a walking, living, multi-miracle with so many testimonies of God's healing power and purpose. She almost died in 1969, when a tubal pregnancy ruptured. She had a terrible car accident in the 1980s. She broke a leg and ankle, and the steering wheel was embedded against her midsection and did a lot of damage. They had to remove her spleen. She was hospitalized for several weeks. She has had congestive heart failure. Her kidneys shut down in 2010, and I didn't think she would make it. She was on hospice in 2014 for kidney failure and congestive heart failure. We were told that she was not doing well and wouldn't make it. We thought each day would be her last. She got down with a bad hip that needed replacing when she was in her late 70s, and the doctor kept putting off the surgery until she got to where she could not go in. Her health bottomed out for months on hospice. She would look daily like she wasn't going to make it. Her daughters, our older sister, and I were trying to care for her. We all had problems with our backs, and we had no choice but to put her in the nursing home. They got her medicine on track and her blood sugar under control. When she started improving, she said, "I'm going to get myself a new hip, and I'm going home." After strength therapy, she went and got a new hip. When she was almost finished with physical therapy, it got infected. She had another hip replacement, and then she got blood poisoning in her leg—more surgery. She had two hip surgeries in about five months' time and three rough therapies. She went into a coma for four days. They told us she was a goner. There was nothing more they could do. Guess what? She came out of it. She said, "God's not finished with me yet." Her kidneys had shut down. They did three weeks of dialysis. They started back working but after time shut down again. Her heart was failing. She had surgery of heart ablation twice to help the function of her heart. The doctor said it would buy her a little time, but they could not fix her heart. She went back to the nursing home for therapy, then dialysis. She finally went back to her apartment. She was living alone and driving for a while. She was still going to dialysis. After three falls, she moved to a wonderful, assisted living. She is still on dialysis three times a week but living and testifying and walking every day with her walker—a little too fast some days. Her mind gets confused sometimes, but she is amazing. She says, "I'm not going any-where until God is through with me." He still uses her every day. She loves to testify about her God. She loves God and her family and most everyone she meets. She's still here smil-ing in 2020 at eighty-three years old. We praise God for her. I so love her smiling face, quick wit, and strong faith in God.

"Worship the Lord with gladness; come before him with joyful songs" (Psalm 100:2 NIV).

"Give praise to the Lord, proclaim his name; make known among the nations what he has done. Sing to him, sing praise to him; tell of all his wonderful acts" (Psalm 105:1-2 NIV).

"Know therefore that the Lord your God is God; he is the faithful God, keeping his covenant of love to a thousand generations of those who love him and keep his commandments" (Deuteronomy 7:9 NIV).

MY YOUNG FRIEND CHRIS

I have a young friend co-worker who is a big lump of sugar, with a heart as big as Texas and Jesus lives there. He is kind, respectful, loving, and has little boy rottenness all rolled up in one funny guy. He struggled with anxiety and insecurities, as we all do, and although he loves Jesus, he's not yet sure who he is in Him. I believe our loving, heavenly Father sent him to work with me so I can encourage him and hopefully get him back in church and reading the Word. The first week we worked together, he told me God was speaking to him through me. I pray he keeps listening and that he hears from God. He loves animals and the outdoors and would love to be a photographer of wildlife. I hope his dream comes true. He has a very sensitive heart and feels the pain of others. He would be good at many things, but I pray for his sake that he will always walk in the footsteps of Jesus, where he will never be misled. I love you, little buddy, and thank God for your smiling face, your wit, and your friendship.

> "Dear friends, let us love one another, for love comes from God. Everyone who loves has been born of God and knows God" (1 John 4:7 NIV).

"However, as it is written: "What no eye has seen, what no ear has heard, and what no human mind has conceived"—the things God has prepared for those who love him" (1 Corinthians 2:9 NIV).

"Love does no harm to a neighbor. Therefore love is the fulfillment of the law" (Romans 13:10 NIV).

"As the Father has loved me, so have I loved you. Now remain in my love" (John 15:9 NIV).

"Jesus replied, 'Anyone who loves me will obey my teaching. My Father will love them, and we will come to them and make our home with them'" (John 14:23 NIV).

FRIENDS

I'm so thankful for friends. They are a gift of sunshine in our lives. The Holy Spirit should be our best friend. I pray that He lives, breathes, and loves through me daily, but I sure love the mixture of people in my life that I work with, go to church with, and meet in places as we travel through life. What would life be without them? They come, and they go. Some are in our lives but for a mere moment, but they leave a sweet, sweet fragrance and a beautiful memory. Some are with us for a lifetime, but all of them were meant to be there. I love the memories—big ones and small ones, the laughs, cups of tea and coffee. Doing life is better with friends. If you don't have any, go make some. In the course of this life, there is so much give and take that it often seems out of balance. God puts people in our lives to help us and people we are to help. Most people we meet in life add something. We learn and grow through the people we meet. Satan also sends people into our lives to distract us and slow us down to delay or stop God's plans. We need to pray for guidance to see the big picture. I have missed it so many times. I'm so thankful for God's grace and mercy. He doesn't give up on us.

> "But the fruit of the Spirit [the result of
> His presence within us] is love [unselfish
> concern for others], joy, [inner] peace,

patience [not the ability to wait, but how we act while waiting], kindness, goodness, faithfulness," (Galatians 5:22 AMP).

"Until now you have not asked [the Father] for anything in My name; but now ask and keep on asking and you will receive, so that your joy may be full and complete" (John 16:24 AMP).

"A happy heart is good medicine and a joyful mind causes healing, But a broken spirit dries up the bones" (Proverbs 17:22 AMP).

THE SPIRIT OF SUICIDE

There are suicidal demons rampant on the Earth today. Suicides are occurring in all age groups and in alarming numbers. If you're a child of God, you have the spirit of the living God within you and the resurrection power of Jesus Christ. Don't be afraid of the demons. They are afraid of you. Know that you have the power to cast them back to the outer darkness in the name of Jesus Christ. Last week there was a young husband and father of three children doing some work in my house. When you walk in the house, you know, I love Jesus. He is represented everywhere, and I can't talk without talking about Him. The young man said before he left, "I'm not supposed to do this, but will you pray for my wife? She's home raising three kids every day and doesn't get to get out much. I work two jobs so she can be home with our kids, but it's hard on her, and she gets suicidal sometimes. Please pray for her." I put out my hands, and he took them. I thanked God that his wife had a loving husband who would ask a stranger to pray for her, and we interceded for her and their family. This is a Christian mother, but she is being attacked by the enemy of her soul. He wants to distract her from putting greatness in her children. He's probably telling her, "Look at what you are missing out on sitting here all day." She might be raising the next Billy Graham or a president, a great missionary, or a doctor who will find great cures for disease and cancer. She doesn't know what a privilege it is to be raising three beautiful children to know and live and do great things for God. She's doing very important work for the kingdom. She takes her kids to church. You don't need to be a businesswoman, turn cartwheels, or jump through hoops. There's time for all that later. She is doing the important part now. I do not intend, in any way, to undermine working mothers. I was one too—no choice, but the more quality time you get with your kids, the better. I used to have a friend, we both lived in army housing, and we traded babysitting so we could get out occasionally. We both had two kids about the same age, and some Bible studies provided a sitter. That's great when you can have that, but get out when the weather is permitting with your kids and enjoy the sunshine, or even take a walk in the rain with them on warm days. I fought that suicidal demon for years before I realized who I was in Christ and that I had power over it. Jesus took on the devil with the cross so we wouldn't have to battle him. Call the prayer partner or the ministry number. Talk to someone, and they will pray with you. 24/7 prayer lines: 1–800–700–7000 or 1-800–731–1000

> Lord Jesus, give strength to Your people and send help. Bless all the parents as they raise their children in this broken world. Give wisdom, knowledge, and strength.

> "Stay alert! Watch out for your great enemy, the devil. He prowls around like a roaring lion, looking for someone to devour" (1 Peter 5:8 NLT).

The End of the Story

In many of my stories, I've spoken of my ex-husband, the father of my children, and the battles we had as the enemy of our souls came against us. The demons he battled cost us all dearly. His father died from a brain tumor when he was one year old, leaving him and his siblings with a void in their lives. He was raised by a Godly mother who kept him in church until he was a teen. As a young boy, he went through sexual abuse, and the abuser taunted and shamed him until this battered little boy told no one. The pain and shame were relentless, and as an early teen, he was introduced to alcohol and pot. He finally found something that eased the pain, having no idea what it would cost him. At the time I met him, he really tried to give it all up, and he did well for a couple of years. As life and work became more stressful, he picked up the alcohol again, and with it that time came violence and adultery. He would stay sober a short while, occasionally a year, then back down that road again. After ten years in the military, he was discharged because of alcoholism and became convinced that it was bigger than he was able to overcome. After his mother's death, he became homeless. It was hard for all of us. We did what we could for him. Then came lung cancer, and the military helped him get benefits and off the streets. Then came brain cancer, a large tumor. He survived the surgery and strong radiation treatment. The nursing home was where he lived after the brain tumor. Then more lung cancer. He fought a hard, painful battle, but as his mind sobered up, he once again found his relationship with the Father and his love for the Word of God. I never doubted his salvation. He could take you to the place where he was saved and baptized. He knew the Word of God. I loved him, and he loved his family and me. As we all know, hurting people hurt people, and when alcohol and drugs are involved, it becomes serious. When it does, it's time to get yourself and your children away safe. He fought a hard battle and, on July 16, 2020, went to be with his Lord and Savior Jesus Christ, who never gave up on him. We had all forgiven him, and he had forgiven his abuser. As his sister sang over him, he peacefully eased into eternity. His battle is over. He is finally living free from all the pain and addictions of this short physical existence and enjoying his spiritual eternity with all his loved ones that have gone on before.

We will all be together again one day. Forevermore.

> "And the peace of God, which passeth all understanding, shall keep your hearts and minds through Christ Jesus" (Philippians 4:7 KJV).

OUR PRAYERS
LIVE FOREVER

Many years ago, I was in a church one Sunday morning, praying at the altar for my lost loved ones. The Lord spoke to me and said, "I am still answering your mother's prayers today. Prayers are forever around my throne." Your prayers never die. Praise God; He's such a wonderful Father, Savior, and Friend.

BELIEVE

As I was working on this book one night, the Lord asked me, "What do you want the reader to take away from reading this book?" I want the readers to know that Jesus Christ is everything that the Word of God says He is. He can do everything the Word says He can do. He will do all the Word says He will when we believe. He is the Living Word. The Word says, "all things are possible to those who believe" (Mark 9:23). What does "all" leave out? Nothing. He can do everything but fail. There are people in churches telling people that healing, miracles, and deliverance are not for today—that their time and place have passed. Stay away from those people. Read the Word of God. Believe it. Live by it, and It will work for you. My God is not dead. He is alive in me and all who have given their lives to Him through the power of His Holy Spirit. If He is not alive in you, you are only a prayer away. Don't waste a moment. Call out to Him. Say, "Lord Jesus, I am a sinner in need of a savior. I am tired of doing life my way. Please forgive me of my sins and come into my heart and be my savior.

"This Book of the Law shall not depart
from your mouth, but you shall meditate
in it day and night, that you may observe
to do according to all that is written in it.

For then you will make your way prosperous, and then you will have good success" (Joshua 1:8 ESV).

FATHER GOD IS ON HIS THRONE

The Lord Jesus Christ is sitting at His right side, making intercessions (prayers) for us (Romans 8:34). If we believe and have asked Jesus in our hearts, the Holy Spirit is in us. Praise God. He is the wind beneath our wings, the one who moves faster than light, who is always there for us. Believe. Pray—invite His help daily in your lives. Read the Word. Share it. Walk in it. Ask Him to live, breathe and love through you daily and to let your light shine.

> "In the same way, let your light shine before others, that they may see your good deeds and glorify your Father in heaven" (Matthew 5:16 NIV).

> "For God, who said, 'Let light shine out of darkness,' made his light shine in our hearts to give us the light of the knowledge of God's glory displayed in the face of Christ" (2 Corinthians 4:6 NIV)

> "Take my yoke upon you and learn from me, for I am humble and gentle in heart,

and you will find rest for your souls" (Matthew 11:29 NIV).

"'For I know the plans I have for you,' declares the Lord, 'plans to prosper you and not to harm you, plans to give you hope and a future'" (Jeremiah 29:11 NIV).

"And hope does not put us to shame, because God's love has been poured out into our hearts through the Holy Spirit, who has been given to us" (Romans 5:5 NIV).

To all my brothers and sisters, sons and daughters of the faith, I'm so glad our lives touched. I don't believe any of us met by accident. All of our lives are like a tapestry, interwoven as we do life together. We love, live, grow, learn, and share joy and heartbreaks together. Tell your stories. Even if you never publish them, write them down for the next generation. We never know how one of our stories will change someone's life. Someone will read them. May the footprints that we leave lead others to believe. The lives we live show them faith. Let them see what Jesus looks like through your eyes. You might tell a story in a way they can relate to. The first Christian book I ever read was Corrie ten Boom's, *The Hiding Place*. I lived on my own and didn't have a TV. My sister-in-law Emily brought it and talked me into reading it. It planted a lot of seeds in my heart. Let's plant some seeds every day somewhere. Love and kindness are beautiful gifts. They do till the soil in the heart and soul. I love you all, always and forever, Vickie.

ABOUT THE AUTHOR

I was born in Naples, Florida, in 1952, to a sawmill fore-man, Clyde, and his stay-at-home wife, Pearl. I was child number ten out of thirteen. There were nine girls and four boys. By the time I was eight, we had lived in Florida twice, Alabama, Tennessee, and three places in Georgia. We settled in Dalton, Georgia, when I was eight years old. Other than the ten years my husband was in the army, North Georgia has been home. I was in church, always, until age ten. Then where we lived, there wasn't one close enough to walk to. I was out of church mostly until the age of twenty-four, when I met Jesus Christ and gave my heart to Him in September of 1976. Jesus, my two children, and grandchildren are the loves of my life. I love cooking and watching people enjoy food. Table time with family and friends is so important. I love a good book, a good Christian movie, and I have found I like to write. Father has been trying for years to get me to write this book, so I know my stories are going to encourage a few lives. That is my prayer. I am loving life with Jesus, family, and friends, cooking Sunday dinners, and working on another book. Love and blessings to you and yours, Vickie.

CPSIA information can be obtained
at www.ICGtesting.com
Printed in the USA
LVHW032327220421
685284LV00005B/40